Bankrupt and Dead:
The Wilma Bailey Story

A Novel

By
Frederick Norment
&
W.R. Schofield

Preface

Call it fate. Call it divine intervention. Call it destiny. Something brought us together. Frederick was a 56 year old award-winning chef. I was a 21 year old student at the University of Michigan. At first, it seemed that the only thing we had in common was that we lived in the same apartment complex. When Frederick barbecued, the whole neighborhood was invited, he just asked that you bring your own plate to fill. When I came with my plate, I had no idea that our collective paths would converge and set us on a trajectory toward fueling both of our creative passions.

After I told Frederick I was studying film, his immediate question was: "Could you help me write my story?" I hesitated. All I wanted to specialize in film school was screenwriting, but I was not yet formally trained. I told him I could do it because I knew the class I was taking next semester would teach me how. I did not realize that Frederick spent his whole life writing, but he had not yet tackled his life story. He told me his mother's story and I was hooked. I was surprised when I realized how the Civil Rights movement negatively affected African American entrepreneurs in the city of Detroit and other major cities around the nation. Wilma Bailey's salon was the epicenter in which to tell this story. This would be the premise of our first screenplay together.

After five drafts of the script, we felt that the best way to tell Frederick's mother's story was through a novel. We believe that our partnership is not only unique but fruitful because of how we've closed a generational gap through writing. This book is a collusion of the perspective of an African American man growing up in Detroit during one of the most chaotic periods in American history and the perspective of a Caucasian young adult who grew up in the same very suburbs that black entrepreneurs abandoned their businesses to flock to. But Wilma Bailey was one of the business owners who did not leave and her dramatic story is one worth telling. Enjoy.

Chapter 1: 1940-1950

The "one-drop rule" was an American colloquial term used for socially classifying an individual as a "Negro" if they had any African ancestry, or more literally, had "one drop of Negro blood" in their genetic makeup. This racial rule deemed 18-year-old Wilma Bailey a Negro woman, yet her skin was lighter because she was the product of a mother who was half black and half white and a Native American father. As a Cherokee Indian, Wilma's father, Harry, had a darker and almost clay-like skin tone that was easily spotted in a large auditorium, filled with white people. Wilma's older brother Harry Junior and her two younger sisters, Chris and Pet, sat in the auditorium, anxious to see Wilma perform. Wilma's sisters matched her lighter skin tone, but it was not light enough to avoid being subjected to racism and segregation.

It was Wilma's turn to take the stage. Sweat dripped down her face like a leaky faucet. She wiped her brow and opened up the black case she brought on stage. She stared at her reflection in the gold and shiny saxophone. She picked up the instrument slowly and carefully, grasping it like a newfound treasure. Even though she knew her routine frontwards and backwards, she still had stage fright. She was one of the few Negro girls participating in a talent show, surrounded by rural and judgmental white folk.

Wilma walked on stage with a demeanor that conveyed confidence, but with a heartbeat that palpitated with fear. Her solution? Drown out fear with music. She began playing a melodious tune that echoed throughout that high school auditorium. Her eyes were fixated on her moving fingers until she decided to gauge the reactions of the crowd. The director of the talent show was smiling, middle-aged white women were bobbing their heads, and some young white kid playfully rocked in his chair to the sounds emanating from Wilma's saxophone.

Wilma was pleased until she gazed upon Hannah, Evelyn, and Marge. They were three bullies in the school who would do whatever it took to bring people down, especially "Negroes." At the same time, all three of them put slices of lemon into their mouths and kept their eyes on Wilma. All of their faces scrunched up as their taste buds absorbed the sourness. Wilma felt a tingling sensation in her mouth, as she psychologically tasted the lemon. Her face contorted slightly and her strict timing of her breaths was almost disrupted. Wilma was tenacious and strong. She decided right then and there that she wasn't going to let anyone ruin her performance, especially not some immature brats who probably felt more insecure about their own lousy talents that they ultimately would have to present. Wilma kept playing that saxophone. She no longer tasted a sour lemon but the sweet taste of music that was harmonic. When Wilma finished, applause erupted and it gave her goose bumps.

Wilma did not win at that talent show. A "Shirley Temple looking" girl on the piano ended up taking the grand prize. However, Wilma did walk away with a victory that night; a mental victory. She realized that no matter what she would do in life there would always be "sour faces" trying to bring her down and she could not change that. All she could do was do her best and not let anyone's opinions or negativity hinder her success. She found it humorous that such an epiphany came to her during something as trivial as a high school talent show, but she had to take inspiration when she could get it. The "lemon prank" pulled that night only scratched the surface of how mean white kids could be. What Wilma tried to instill in her siblings was that racism came from fear and acceptance came from hope. Hope was something their family needed more of.

The sound of the applause in the auditorium drowned out the booming thunder outside. As the crowd of people exited the auditorium, their attention was turned to the black sky that had a green tinge to it. There was stillness in the air that made it feel like time was frozen. For any resident of Keokuk, Iowa, it was time to seek shelter. Harry grabbed Wilma's arm tightly.

"Let's get home before it touch down," said Harry gravely.

The members of the Bailey family walked briskly down the street. As the wind blew harder, they walked faster. At the farmhouse, Wilma's stepmother, Claireece, held the screen door shut so it wouldn't blow off the hinges. Behind her stood her and Harry's two toddlers, Bunny and Joanne. Claireece sighed with relief as she gazed upon her husband and the rest of the family run up to the screen door.

"We gotta get to the storm cellar," yelled Harry over the loud gusts of wind.

The family ran to their storm cellar that had been used many times in the past. Food, water, and linens kept them comfortable throughout the night as a tornado roared outside. Harry held his children tight, realizing that this was the longest storm he had ever experienced in his thirty years of living in Iowa. Unlike the film that was released a year before, a tornado would not send anyone to a magical place. It was a life threatening force of nature that, although dangerous, The Bailey family's religious convictions would classify it as God's work. Humans would never understand why. The Bailey family prayed all night in that storm cellar. The children's prayers were answered and their lives were spared. Harry's prayer for minimal damage to his property was not.

The next morning the sun blazed with a brightness that contrasted the dark gloom of yesterday. The Bailey family could not believe what they saw, or more importantly, what they did

not see: the Bailey Farmhouse. The house where Wilma's mom

would read her bedtime stories every night. The house that

brought their Midwestern family together for the holidays, and

the house that Wilma's mom died in when she was only ten years

old, was no more. For a second, Wilma fooled herself into

thinking the house did go to that magical place, but all of the cow

corpses sprawled all over the farm and the striking visual of

splinters lodged into a stone, brought her back to reality. Harry

looked at his land in shock.

"Lord knows, I'm a God fearing man, but kids, I can't

take it anymore. We're moving to Michigan. Your aunt has a

farm there," said Harry defiantly.

The move to Michigan would not be such a positive

change for the family, as Harry would have expected. The

weather was less dangerous, but the conditions for his offspring

were not ideal. On a beautiful spring day, Harry Junior was riding

on the floorboard of a 1925 Ford Roundabout pickup truck while

his reckless friend was behind the wheel. They sped through the woods near Romulus, Michigan swerving between the trees. Harry Junior did not hold on tight enough during the sharpest turn. He was thrown off the truck and flew head first into a tree. He died instantly. Chris' life in Michigan became more miserable compared to Iowa. She got involved in a dysfunctional relationship with an abusive boyfriend that ultimately led to her death. After a big argument with her boyfriend, the drunken bastard struck her while she was in the shower. She fell and hit her head.

Pet's fate was similar to that of her siblings. In her 30s, she became pregnant and was unable to afford the child, like many women in America faced with an impossible situation. With no Planned Parenthood or safer options, she turned to the street. She begrudgingly sought out a "back-alley" abortion to terminate the pregnancy. She hemorrhaged until she passed away. Unbeknownst to a young Wilma, these tragedies would give her the inner strength and tenacity she needed in order to create a more positive future.

Through her adolescence, Wilma loved creating music,

vocally and instrumentally. But her love for music was not her primary passion. What made Wilma the most vivacious was styling hair. She loved making people feel beautiful no matter what they looked like or who they were. A head of hair was a head of hair and Wilma did not discriminate against anyone. Not that she even had the option to discriminate as a student of the Michigan College of Beauty. Before coming to cosmetology school, Wilma had only been a master of her younger sister's hair and the coarse hair of the neighbors that lived down the road, but now she was an expert in all types of hair; thick and wavy, thin and stringy, short and long.

It was her last week of school and she had already established a reputation for herself as one of the most detail-oriented and talented hair stylists. This cultivated jealousy and resentment from her white lady colleagues, but Wilma ignored their "sour faces" like she always did. Wilma had just finished styling the hair of none other than the School President herself. Priscilla was a middle-aged white woman, who dressed to impress and always expected the best from her students. Wilma stood anxiously as Priscilla studied herself in the mirror, taking note of all the curls and silkiness that Wilma had created.

"Hudson's is offering you a job," said Priscilla flatly.

"Hudson's?" asked Wilma incredulously.

"Yes, J.L. Hudson's. Do you want me to spell the whole thing out for you?"

Wilma could not contain her excitement. She had not even graduated and she already had a job offer, at Hudson's nonetheless. The J.L. Hudson Company was a prominent retail department store in Detroit. The flagship store on Woodward Avenue was one of the tallest department stores in the world at the time with a bustling lobby full of hair stylists and makeup artists that did what they did best. Since her family moved to a farm in Grass Lake, Michigan, Wilma had only experienced Detroit from her commutes to and from cosmetology school. Now there would be no more structured curriculum but actually working in the great city of Detroit. The future just banged on her door. It was time for her to answer.

Six months had passed since taking the job at Hudson's

and her disillusionment with the company set in. Wilma soon realized that she was recruited as a novelty more so than a stylist. Hudson's goal was to increase their profitability by getting more Negro clients and Wilma was the key. Sometimes the key didn't fit in the lock. Wilma would be lucky to style two clients a day. She would spend hours watching affluent white women walk passed her, afraid to even make eye contact. And the ones who did would usually scoff at her. Although she did not take these instances personally, she knew it was bad for business. Wilma was not making as much as she wanted and she felt trapped. It was not until a middle-aged woman named Doris approached her that made Wilma feel more enthusiastic about her passion again. Doris was a short, Negro woman with black curled hair and a smile that was infectious. She met Wilma at her workstation and started conversation.

"I've been watching you, Wilma Bailey," said Doris.

"Should I be concerned?" asked Wilma jokingly.

"Only if you think admiring talent is wrong."

"Who are you, exactly?" asked Wilma curiously.

"My name is Doris. I own a salon on Grand River and I would like to offer you a job."

Was this divine intervention? thought Wilma.

Just as Wilma thought about her listlessness with Hudson's, an angel in the form of a Negro woman swooped down with another offer. But Wilma did not want to appear too excited. She needed to stay grounded before making any rash comments or decisions.

"I'm not sure. I've only been here six months."

"Our people aren't coming here. They come to my shop. You're lucky to get one or two white people to have the courage to sit in your chair in a place like this."

If Wilma learned anything about Doris was that she talked straight. She "told it how it was." Although one might consider Doris' stalking of Wilma as something unorthodox, it did convey that she was driven. She wanted the best stylists and Wilma was starting to realize that she was one of the best. Wilma still had her doubts.

"You know I don't have clientele yet," said Wilma.

"Wilma, I got so many walk-ins a day. They will be your new clientele. Just think about it."

Doris gave Wilma her card and left the spacious lobby. Wilma looked at her coworkers. Mostly everyone had a client and they were happy, conversing and styling. Wilma stood their awkwardly as more potential clients walked passed her. It felt like her life was walking passed her in that moment. She was not targeting the Negro market in the best way she could. Doris was right about Hudson's.

Our people aren't coming here...

It was impulsive, but that night Wilma quit Hudson's and called Doris. Wilma would start her new job next week.

Chapter 2: 1963 (Part One)

The year was 1963. It was a year that began with the spewing of inflammatory rhetoric that seemed to catch the whole nation on fire. On January 14, newly elected Governor of Alabama, George Wallace conveyed his desire to maintain a certain "status quo" in his inaugural address. His declaration: "Segregation today, segregation tomorrow, segregation forever!" was a poignant representation of the racial tensions of the time.

Four months later, thousands of Negroes protested these "Jim Crow" laws in the city of Birmingham, which prompted Public Safety Commissioner Eugene "Bull" Connor to unleash fire hoses and police dogs on the demonstrators. Reflected through the new medium of television, it was racists like Wallace and "Bull," and the atrocities that surrounded them, that ultimately gave more power to the budding Civil Rights Movement. A movement that would empower Negro citizens like never before with regards to fair housing, voting, and being treated like equals.

Detroit, Michigan had a lot more open-minded people

compared to Birmingham, Alabama. Negro entrepreneurship skyrocketed in the 1960s and prosperity was the common theme. There was no more segregation or "separate but equal" nonsense. It was a city of dreams for Negroes that could commerce with each other like never before. They owned gas stations, supermarkets, and beauty salons.

For Detroit, June 11, 1963 was a spring day like any other. The sun shined and the flowers bloomed in the places where the urban landscape had not yet expanded. A large white flower hung from a branch of a Dogwood tree next to a street sign that read "Woodward Avenue." A gust of wind blew the flower off of the tree, making it dance gracefully in the air before lying to rest on the pavement. The engine of a white Cadillac, constructed only a few months prior, roared as its respective vehicle raced down the street. The tires crushed the flower right as the brakes screeched loudly making the car come to an abrupt stop. The driver was John L., a 32-year-old, dark-skinned Negro man, who wore a red sharkskin suit. John L. had a commanding presence about him. He clutched the wheel with one hand wearing a bright gold carrot ring and he smoked a cigar in the other hand. His dark, determined eyes and stoic expression on his face conveyed to anyone that saw him that he was a man of confidence, even if it wasn't put to use in the most morally constructive way. In the passenger seat sat Doreetha, a 30-year-old woman matching the same skin tone as John L. Her curvy and voluptuous body barely fit into a black mini skirt and red fishnets. Her aura screamed promiscuity coupled with an attitude of carelessness. They complemented each other well, in appearances anyway.

"Get that money for us, baby. Make me proud," John L. said to Doreetha.

He proceeded to give her a long kiss on the lips that was interrupted by the high-pitched yelp of Dexter, a standard poodle dyed the same bright red color of John L.'s suit. The dog popped his head out from the back seat giving a menacing look that indicted his master for paying more attention to Doreetha than him. Doreetha glared at Dexter and exited the car.

"Dexter, let's find some bitches!" declared John L. as he

revved his engine, causing Dexter to bark continuously.

John L. turned on his radio. "Night Train" by James Brown played loudly.

"All aboard!" yelled John L. over the blaring music.

John L. sped down Woodward away from a sauntering Doreetha whose sparkling red high heels clacked as she meandered down the street, hips swinging back and forth like a pendulum. A multitude of women wearing equally as revealing clothes surrounded the area. The black heels of one of the prostitutes rushed across Woodward to a potential client that pulled up in a Lincoln. Her high heels poked a hole through the now crushed and blackened Dogwood flower.

Appearances. John L. wore his sharkskin suit to represent his "larger than life" appearance. Doreetha flaunted her attractive body in skimpy clothes to promote her "looking for a good time?" appearance. On the opposite side of the spectrum was Wilma, whose appearance mirrored her independence through a blonde streak worn in the middle of her short black hair. In 1963, she was 40 years old but did not look a day over 30. She stood as a sharp contrast to the short and haggard Asian woman she was talking to in the salon backroom. Kim was the exact opposite of Wilma, in appearances and personality. Wilma enjoyed being in the spotlight as the face of Bailey's Salon. Kim preferred isolationism. Her job was to make and style all of the wigs in the backroom. Kim tended to complain about everything that bothered her: wig shipments being late, other co-workers giving her a hard time, and not getting paid what she felt she "deserved" among other things.

"Everything is gonna be all right," Wilma said to Kim in her calming and soothing voice.

"I use all wigs on Motown. No hair left," Kim retorted frantically.

Although Kim liked to complain, this particular complaint was legitimate. The stars and clients of Detroit's own Motown Records made up one of Wilma's largest accounts generating high profits. Many of the female singers wore wigs during their performances. Thus there were a lot of wigs going in and out of the salon for Kim to color, curl, and style. If all the wigs in a shipment went out to Motown, that left none for the "day to day clients" during normal business hours. Wilma knew that any transactions affiliated with Motown superseded any regular client that entered her salon, but Wilma felt the need to appease Kim, who, although a pain in the ass, was an asset to the salon.

"I'll have Kathy pick up more from Diggs," Wilma said as she eyed Kim's messy workstation.

"Wilma!" a high pitched, flamboyant voice cried from the salon.

Wilma exited the backroom, to the spacious and busy salon. Stylists Kathy and Anita, attractive Negro women, in their thirties, who could pass for twins, did the nails of their respective clients on the left side of the salon. On the right side of the room, was Moe, a 35-year-old, white, chunky yet muscular man, on his knees fixing a jukebox with a screwdriver. He was the only white face in a sea of black but it didn't seem to bother him as he worked diligently. Next to Moe and the jukebox worked Janette, a woman with a dark complexion, who shared the same age as Wilma but not her looks. Janette stood over an attractive Negro woman named Ruby, who was seated in one of the salon chairs. Both of them stared at Ruby's hairstyle in the mirror. Bryce, a 29-year-old, tall, and skinny man was sweeping the floor until Janette's work on Ruby caught his attention. Bryce made eye contact with the newly arrived Wilma.

"Wilma, we need you over here," shouted the same flamboyant voice, which emanated from Bryce's squeaky windpipes.

Wilma walked toward Bryce, hiding her annoyance with him for the sake of maintaining her professional appearance in front of the clients.

"Wilma, please correct Lady Janette over here before she commits some hair heresy!"

Bryce liked to exaggerate everything. His flair for the dramatic entertained most of the clients yet bothered most of the workers. He always thought he was right and would argue with anyone who told him otherwise. There was a thin line between confidence and conceit, and Bryce rarely knew where it was.

Janette tolerated Bryce and was one of the few workers

who had the most patience with him. Janette was all about being the best stylist she could be even if it meant learning something new from a boisterous Bryce or a wise Wilma to make her better.

"Is that not how you did Miss Ross' hair last week?" inquired Janette.

"I want Miss Ross to notice me in the crowd tonight!" blurted an excited Ruby.

Wilma smiled and leaned over a seated Ruby to examine her hairstyle as Bryce leaned over Wilma anxiously, putting his weight on one leg. Wilma proceeded to convey her expertise.

"You're close but..."

"The wave has to be more to the right, slightly above the eye," interrupted Bryce.

Wilma turned and glared at Bryce. Bryce shrugged his shoulders and smiled cockily, knowing he was right. Wilma turned back to Janette who looked at Wilma for validation of Bryce's impulsive declaration.

"Yes. Right about here," sighed Wilma.

Wilma pointed to a part of Ruby's forehead. Janette

nodded decisively and began to curl Ruby's hair following Wilma's instructions.

"Next step; sing on stage!" said Ruby passionately.

"I'd go see you," said Janette warmly.

Bryce smirked and went back to sweeping, appearing to be done interfering with anyone else's business. Wilma walked over to Kathy and Anita, still doing their manicures.

"Kathy, tomorrow before you come in, could bring back more hair from Diggs?" asked Wilma.

"Of course," replied Kathy.

Kathy was the youngest stylist who looked up to Wilma and was always quick to make her life easier. Anita was a little older and tended to keep to herself, but whenever there was an opportunity for a joke, she'd chime in.

"Wigs from Diggs. Fresh off the head of the dead!" said Anita jokingly.

Sometimes the jokes didn't land.

"You use hair from a funeral home?" asked Anita's client concernedly.

Anita paused from polishing, knowing she revealed a salon secret. She looked up at Wilma, whose face said: "Really, Anita?" Kathy needed to end this awkward silence.

"That, and horsehair," declared Kathy.

The client's eyes bulged. Anita chuckled. Wilma thought about neutralizing the situation by explaining to the "bug eyed" client that the hair was washed and that the process was sanitary, but Wilma knew that Kathy and Anita's clients were loyal and would still come for their weekly appointments no matter which controversial place Wilma plucked hair from.

In the back of the salon, Wilma's young sons: Ricky and Ronnie played which was often synonymous with "roughhousing" and "smack talking."

"Bibble bobble, when he walks his titties wobble," sneered Ronnie.

Ronnie was Wilma's oldest son who was 11 years old in 1963. He was a skinny boy who enjoyed making fun of his younger brother's chubbiness. But Ronnie wasn't kind on the eyes himself. His chin was disfigured from a failed operation during his youth. For Ronnie, being called "crooked face" and being demoralized by bullies on a day-to-day basis was normal. It was refreshing for Ronnie to be the bully for once, even if it meant making his younger brother the victim. But Ricky would always defend himself. Especially now that his older brother said he had little man boobs. This would not stand. Ricky lunged at Ronnie fiercely and as fast as his heavier body could take him. Ronnie quickly latched his arm around Ricky's neck putting him in a headlock.

"Ronnie, leave me alone. Mommy!" cried Ricky.

"Little sissy," said Ronnie snidely.

Ricky was a "Mama's Boy." who tended to use maternal intervention to end a lot of the conflicts with his brother. In 1963, he was seven years old and chubbier than most kids his age. He just loved his mother's food so much. He enjoyed cooking with Wilma and watching her style hair in awe. One could argue that Ricky was Wilma's biggest fan next to Kathy.

"Enough!" yelled Wilma as she broke them apart. Ricky grunted. Ronnie smirked.

"Ronnie, fill up the soda machine."

Wilma pulled out a set of keys from her pocket and threw them at Ronnie. He caught them with ease and made his way to the Pepsi soda machine by the jukebox. Repairman Moe got a closer look at Ronnie's chin. He examined it for a couple seconds before Ronnie's dashing gaze struck Moe like lightning. Ronnie's instincts of people staring at him got stronger as he got older. But becoming more noticeable to criticism didn't make it any less difficult to deal with.

"Ricky, turn off the television," commanded Wilma.

Ricky nodded and walked over to the television set against the back wall, more self conscious of how his body looked as he was moving. On the television screen was President Kennedy who addressed the nation from the Oval Office regarding his decision to send in The National Guard to protect two Negro students and escort them safely into the University of Alabama, much to Governor George Wallace's dismay.

Ricky stopped and listened to the President, a man he admired for his charisma.

"We preach freedom around the world, and we mean it, and we cherish our freedom here at home, but are we to say to the world, and much more importantly, to each other that this is a land of the free except for the Negroes; that we have no second-class citizens except Negroes; that we have no class or cast system, no ghettos, no master race except with respect to Negroes?"

"Ricky!" shouted Wilma from across the salon.

Ricky snapped out of it and turned off the television. No one seemed to care or notice. Across the salon, a sweaty Moe stood up and walked toward Wilma.

"Jukebox is fixed, Wilma."

"Thanks, Moe. Tell him I'll call Friday."

Moe nodded and left the salon, carrying his toolbox. Ronnie gave him a menacing look that Moe didn't notice at all. Ronnie apathetically continued stocking the soda machine with bottles of Pepsi. Wilma pulled out a quarter and flicked it at an oncoming Ricky. Ricky, who had less hand eye coordination than Ronnie, dropped the quarter but was able to scoop it up quite quickly.

"Play a song, baby," said Wilma.

Ricky skipped to the now working jukebox and inserted the quarter.

"Heat Wave" by Martha Reeves & The Vandellas blared. The whole shop came to life as Ricky starting doing "The Twist" in the middle of the shop. The clients threw loose change at his dancing feet, which seemed to be a ritual for the salon and a lucrative source of income for young Ricky. In 1963, a quarter could buy two candy bars, a bag of chips, and a twelve-ounce soda or five Reese's Cups. For a chubby boy like Ricky, that was a difficult decision to make.

"Shake those hips, Ricky!" yelled Anita.

The clients and workers laughed and sang along. The only one not having fun was Ronnie, who still had a lot of bottles to put into the machine. The entrance bell rang but no one heard it over the loud music. Moreover, it was the entrance of a hobbling Lawrence that attracted the attention of the salon patrons. Lawrence was a short and elderly man who always wore a brown jacket, no matter what temperature it was outside. He called it his safety vest, which kept him safe from something only Lawrence knew and never explained further. Janette and Kathy both acknowledged Lawrence and greeted him. He stood at the front counter for Wilma, who was distracted by her dancing son in the middle of the salon.

"Wilma, come take my number! And turn down that music, I can't hear shit," shouted Lawrence.

Wilma smiled and walked over to the counter giving her grumpy friend her undivided attention.

"What'll it be today, Lawrence?"

"Wilma, I want fifty cent on 321."

"That money roll, huh?" asked Wilma.

"You know it."

"All right baby, good luck and don't forget to tip the boss," joked Wilma.

"Of course, Wilma. I've got to come get my money, right?

Initially, Wilma wasn't keen on running the numbers

from her shop. She was raised in a small town with righteous values instilled in her at a young age so for her to partake in such an illegal affair, at times, made her uncomfortable. But she always went back to the thought:

I'm not hurting anyone so it's fine.

If anything, she believed she was giving a lot of poor folk hope by offering this opportunity for them to make some real money. Running the numbers also gave her shop more exposure and notoriety and that definitely wasn't bad for business.

"Take care, everyone," said Lawrence.

He walked out of the salon slowly into the dusk of Detroit. Lawrence breathed in deeply and admired the peaceful intersection of Glendale and Linwood. There wasn't any traffic and only a few civilians roamed the streets. Just as Lawrence stopped smelling the roses, or dogwood flowers that bloomed outside the buildings, the roaring engine of John L.'s Cadillac pierced the peace. John L. joyously sped down Linwood until he slammed on his brakes and parked in front of a spacious window that read "Bailey's Salon" painted in large red letters. Lawrence glared at John L. and shook his head in disgust at this young "pimp" who Lawrence regarded as a disgrace to their race. John L. got out of the car, not giving Lawrence the time of day. He let Dexter out of the back seat and the dog wandered around the street, sniffing everything. The dog shat at the base of the Dogwood tree on Wilma's property.

John L., with Dexter at his feet, entered the salon. This time the bell connected to the door was more audible now that the music was softer and Ricky had ceased dancing to rest in a salon chair. An excitable Dexter became the new source of entertainment for the salon patrons. Dexter felt the need to sniff every person in the salon. Bryce ignored the dog only to size up John L. with a wanting gaze. Wilma approached John L.

"You look...colorful," said Wilma.

She hugged her younger cousin. John L. kissed Wilma on the cheek.

"Looks like business is good, Wilma."

"What have you been up to?" asked Wilma.

"Living The Dream."

A rambunctious Dexter returned to his master's feet. Wilma got on her knees and pet the dog, whose fur matched John L.'s red pant leg and shoe quite perfectly.

"You're so cute you, little fire ball, you," said Wilma in a tone that any human being would find condescending.

"That's Dexter," said John L.

"You do like it here," commented Wilma.

John L.'s favorite street was Dexter Avenue. He had only lived in Detroit for a little while, but had already built up quite the reputation as a "no-nonsense" pimp that always got what he wanted. Wilma knew of John L.'s lifestyle and didn't agree with it. She also knew that as a Negro during this time period, sometimes the morally questionable careers were the only ones that could make a comfortable living. It wasn't like her business started purely so why should she judge. John L. would always be her cousin and a Miller. Millers and Baileys looked out for each other. That's how Wilma thought anyway.

Kim swung open the backroom door swiftly. She wore a yellow coat and a matching handbag on her wrist. She walked briskly toward the counter and stopped.

"No hair. No work," stated Kim.

"The hair will be here bright and early tomorrow, Kim," said Wilma.

Kim gave a decisive nod and then locked eyes with John L., who stared her down like she was prey that needed to be ravaged. Kim left the salon, visibly shaken by John L.'s look.

"You let one of them work here?" asked John L. incredulously.

"You gonna come here and do the wigs?" asked Wilma sarcastically.

Wilma never viewed John L. as racist growing up, but it was when John L. came back from the Korean War, that spurts of racism bubbled up to the surface. To John L., any Asian was a "chink" and not to be trusted. This belief hardened in him after seeing so many of his friends blown away by said "chinks." Whether it was man, woman, or child, to John L., any Asian was a threat. It was a shame that war could poison his perspective of half the world's population. The only cure for this poison was education and understanding, a bitter pill John L. would rather choke on as opposed to swallow.

Dexter's sniffing spree took him to Ronnie who was finishing up stocking the last of the bottles. Dexter smelled Ronnie and licked him on his face. Ronnie was always fond of animals. He was known for stealing pets from the school aquarium and petting zoo and kept their presences hidden from Wilma, with Ricky only stumbling onto them occasionally. Ricky liked the animals too, which trumped his desire to be the "perfect son" and tattle on Ronnie. Distracted by Dexter, Ronnie mindlessly dropped one of the Pepsi bottles on the floor, shattering it. Pepsi flooded the floor.

"Ronnie!" yelled Wilma.

Chapter 3: Spring 1955

It was a spring day in 1955. So far the year had yielded interesting events in American history. There were some significant strides and setbacks for Negroes. The year started off on the right note. Marian Anderson was the first Negro singer to perform at the Metropolitan Opera in New York City. Applause erupted for her before she started singing, which was a testament to the historical significance of the occasion.

A lesser-known heroine of the year was 15 year old Claudette Colvin. Much like Rosa Parks who would do the same later in the year, Colvin refused to give up her seat on a bus in Montgomery, Alabama, to a white woman after the driver demanded it. She was carried off the bus backwards while she was kicked, handcuffed, and harassed on the way to the police station.

It was a rocky road toward equality and in every corner of the nation; Negroes were being taken advantage of. Sometimes it wasn't always physical abuse but financial and emotional abuse as well. For three-year-old Ronnie, it was all of the above. Not many kids can remember events when they were that young, Ronnie had enough trauma that year to last a lifetime.

Doctor Horowitz was a middle-aged white man with messy gray hair littered with dandruff. He was considered one of the best Ear, Nose, and Throat doctors in Detroit at the time. That was part of the reason Ronnie had surgery that spring day. Wilma wanted the best for her son and Doctor Horowitz was supposed embody that. But even great doctors make mistakes or sometimes they make deliberate decisions that may hurt a patient but generate high profits. White doctors siphoning off money from naive Negroes was normal for the time, even in a northern city such as Detroit.

Doctor Horowitz stood over the operating table where Ronnie lay unconscious with a white bandage covering his chin. Nurse Lisa, a short, white woman, with brunette hair, stood loyally next to Horowitz and watched the doctor rub his chin, contemplating what to do next.

"I'll let her know," said Nurse Lisa.

Nurse Lisa began walking toward the door. Doctor

Horowitz grabbed her arm.

"No. I'll tell her," he said with conviction.

Wilma waited anxiously in the corridor of the hospital. In 1955, Wilma was 32 and did not yet have a blonde streak through her black hair. She sat alone shaking her legs nervously.

It's been too long. Something went wrong. I shouldn't have went through with this, she thought.

Doctor Horowitz and Nurse Lisa came out of the patient room. Nurse Lisa lowered her head and walked down the hallway passed Wilma, avoiding eye contact with her. Wilma stood up abruptly and confronted Horowitz.

"How is he?" asked Wilma.

"He's doing just fine."

Wilma looked at him skeptically. "Fine" wasn't good enough. And his tone wasn't very convincing. Her face contorted which prompted Horowitz to delve deeper into Ronnie's condition faster than he originally planned to.

"We had a minor problem," he said bluntly.

Wilma's face dropped. She had been hesitant to go

through with the surgery from the beginning. It was Doctor Horowitz who said it would be an easy procedure and now he was telling her that there was a problem. This utterance made Wilma tremble. Wilma didn't care how minor the problem was when it had to do with her son's well-being. Sleep Apnea, he told her. He could die in his sleep if this surgery wasn't done.

"But don't worry. We cleared the blockage in his trachea. His snoring will no longer affect his breathing," said Horowitz matter-of-factly.

"What happened?" asked Wilma.

"Keep using the Vicks rub and the vapor machine. His face should heal just fine."

"What did you do to my son?" questioned Wilma.

A week and a half later, in her small apartment, Wilma was on her knees, changing the large bandage on Ronnie's face. It was a hard thing to do considering how hysterically Ronnie was crying. She stopped trying and hugged her son tightly.

"It's okay baby, Mama's here. Everything is gonna be all right."

In that moment, the bedroom door swung open loudly. This distracted Ronnie and his crying subsided. It was Ronnie's father and Wilma's husband: Barney. Barney was a 40 year old, dark-skinned man. He held a brown-bagged bottle in his hand and reeked of the beer that was inside of it. His small tee shirt barely covered up his large gut. It was surprising that Ronnie grew up to be so skinny, but drinking five beers a day could fatten up anyone no matter what genes they had.

"What's wrong, Ronnie? You were in that damn hospital for ten days. Didn't that fuckin' Jew fix you up?" said Barney, slurring his words.

Ronnie became silent and nuzzled his face into his mother's stomach. He was clearly frightened by his loud talking father and knew from experience that crying would not be tolerated. Wilma refused to turn and face Barney, hoping his drunkenness would lead him on a quest to find more alcohol as opposed to deal with his "annoying" family. Hope wasn't always enough. Barney stumbled in closer toward Wilma and Ronnie almost as if he was moving in slow motion.

"Let me see him."

"Leave us alone," said Wilma angrily.

"He didn't need it. I told you he didn't need it."

"Go away!" yelled Wilma.

"They put him under the blade just to get your money. Let me see my son."

Slow motion sped up when Barney quickly extended his arm to turn Wilma' body to face him. Wilma let go of Ronnie and pushed Barney forcefully into a dresser, causing him and a lamp to fall down. Wilma picked up Ronnie and ran out of the apartment, down the stairs, and out of the building. Wilma held Ronnie tightly and sprinted down a street in Downtown Detroit.

Wilma had been planning to leave Barney for months. She despised drinking and hated the kind of man he became: a dirty, rude, and lazy man. If Wilma valued anything it was productivity and tenacity and she wanted those values instilled in Ronnie. When she ran through the street with her son, it felt like she was unshackling the bonds of fear that Barney held her to for the last three years. This could be a fresh start for her and Ronnie.

Wilma was not going to let a failed operation and financial stress bring her down. She needed to be strong for herself and her son.

Chapter 4: Summer 1955

A few months had passed since Wilma's defiant decision but not every person of color had the liberty of living in Detroit, where Negroes were rarely treated as second-class citizens. On August 28, 1955, 14-year-old Emmett Till had apparently "flirted" with a white woman in a small grocery store in Money, Mississippi. Such behavior was not tolerated by the local racists and Till was brutally murdered. The eventual trial of the perpetrators lead the Regional Council of Negro Leadership leader, Dr. T.R.M. Howard, to invite black congressman and civil rights activist: Charles Diggs Jr. from Detroit, Michigan. Diggs was the first Negro elected to the Congress in Michigan. He also ran his family's business, The House of Diggs, which was Michigan's largest funeral home at one point as well as a future account for Bailey's Salon. Diggs and Wilma were to become good friends in the coming years and Wilma always admired him for going to Mississippi for such a sensitive and moral cause that would spark the fire of the whole Civil Rights Movement.

Wilma had first met Diggs right after he returned from

Mississippi that summer. Wilma walked around the lobby of the Diggs family funeral home, waiting to be led to the fresh cadavers. She expected to meet with Charles Diggs Senior, the elder Diggs whose frail appearance was apt for a funeral parlor, but instead she met with his younger son. Diggs Jr. came out from the backroom and greeted Wilma.

"Welcome to the House of Diggs, how can I help you?"

"I'm from Doris' salon. I'm here to do the hair."

"I guess somebody has too, huh?"

Wilma did not appreciate his sarcastic tone. It may not have been the most conventional job, but she was happy to do it. How could a body be buried with hair looking like hell? The extra money was a bonus too.

"My boss spoke to Mr. Diggs about coming in today, if this is a bad time..."

"I travel a lot so I'm not always aware of my father's appointments but this way, I'll lead you."

Diggs appeared to be a meek yet focused man. He wore large round glasses that seemed to magnify his eyes. Little did she know, that after hearing what this man had done in Mississippi a month prior, it would shift her perspective of him entirely, at least when it came to admiration and respect. As they walk passed the incinerator, Wilma had a thought that she turned into a vocalized inquiry for Diggs.

"What do you do with the hair from the bodies that are to be cremated?"

After his experiences in college, military, and congress, Diggs thought he heard it all, but his face could not help but contort as he processed the obscure question. Instead of telling the truth that it goes up in smoke with the rest of the body, he thought of a response that she might like better.

"Whatever you want."

Wilma nodded slowly as she considered uses for such hair. Diggs was hoping for some kind of reaction but Wilma kept to herself. Wilma and Diggs entered the backroom in which two bodies of once elderly women were lying on gurneys with pillows propping them up, ready to be styled. The women were already dressed for the viewing, which would be done that evening. Wilma set down her vinyl styling bag on the edge of a nearby counter and got her supplies ready. Wilma placed towels on the shoulders of her new "clients" to avoid staining the nice clothing.

"If you need anything, I'll be in the lobby," said Diggs sincerely.

"A fan and a glass of water would be good. I haven't even started working yet and I'm already sweating."

Although Michigan was known for its bitter winters, the summers were steamier than most people were comfortable with. Later that day in Doris' quaint salon, Wilma and another stylist did the hair of their respective clients. Various table fans blew, but everyone still sweated. Soft piano ballads played on the radio near the front desk. On the wall behind the desk, hung a crucifix and a painting of The Sacred Heart of Jesus. Doris was a devout Christian and had no problem letting people know that. She even believed that if the clients looked long enough at Jesus they would too convert to Christianity and save their souls. Wilma was raised Catholic but didn't practice since she moved to

Detroit. This was a fact she would never reveal to Doris. On the other side of the spectrum was the agnostic Shirley, Wilma's best friend and client Wilma currently worked on as she tried to prevent drops of sweat from raining down on Shirley's head. Shirley was a 33 year old white woman who was slender and well-dressed. Shirley was Wilma's confidant. Their friendship blossomed when Wilma first did Shirley's hair a few years back. Shirley appreciated Wilma's attention to detail and knowledge of cosmetology. In 1955, their paring was a novelty since black women and white women were rarely friends. To some snobbish white folk, Shirley would be considered a "white nigger" for marrying a black man and spending her time around black people more than white people. Shirley dismissed these insults. She always looked on the bright side even if she affiliated herself with "Negroes."

"Are you sure Jerry doesn't mind?" asked Wilma as she curled Shirley's hair.

"Him spending all that time with Ronnie should hold him off from trying to get me pregnant," retorted Shirley.

"Being a mother is difficult, but it has its rewards...It must be nice to have a stay-at-home husband."

"When he's not sitting on his ass counting his money all the time."

"We'll be moving out next week. I can't thank you enough Shirley," said Wilma with sincerity.

"You keep making my hair look this good, and you and Ronnie can stay forever."

The thought of staying with Shirley forever bothered Wilma. She enjoyed Shirley's company and appreciated her opening her home to her and Ronnie, giving her time to get back on her feet, but by the end of the summer, Wilma was determined to get her own place. Her strength of character wouldn't have it any other way. Wilma took off Shirley's apron and made eye contact with her in the mirror that collectively conveyed satisfaction for both of them.

"You're the best in the Midwest, Wilma."

Wilma smiled and walked with Shirley to the front counter. Shirley handed Wilma a stack of cash as Wilma opened the register.

"This is way too much, Shirley."

"Put it towards your shop. I know how much that means to you."

Wilma hesitated for a few seconds but took the money. She put half in the register and half in her pocket. Shirley was always a good tipper but this time was more than usual. It perplexed Wilma but she decided it wasn't worth the real estate in her mind. She was just lucky to have such a good friend in her corner.

"Just promise me that your shop will play some good music instead of this elevator bullshit," said Shirley.

"Shirley, you wouldn't know good music if it started playing down from the Heavens," spewed Doris as she exited the backroom of the salon.

"Your Guardian Angel must be deaf," sneered Shirley.

"At least I have a Guardian Angel. They gave up on your ass long ago."

"I'm pretty sure swearing is a sin, replied Shirley."

The black woman stylist and client nearby held back their laughter. Banter between Shirley and Doris was always comedic but there was something deeper underlying in it. They both subtly competed for Wilma's soul...at least that's how Doris' religious mind viewed her relationship with Shirley. Doris often considered herself the "Angel" on Wilma's shoulder while Shirley was "The Devil" on the other. Why else would Shirley diminish Doris when she read scripture to Wilma or always wear that dark red lipstick? Doris didn't always connect the dots in the right direction, but she was always a good judge of character and to her, Shirley was bad news. She just wished Wilma saw that too.

"We're going to Chubby's tonight. And we're gonna dance and we're gonna have fun," declared Shirley to Wilma.

"You know I don't have fun at those places," admitted Wilma.

"How else do you expect to meet men, Wilma? It's just like Butter Ball says, it's not the size of the ship, it's the motion of the ocean."

Shirley and Wilma busted out laughing with a few chuckles coming from the other salon patrons. Doris looked at Shirley with disdain, knowing that Shirley already won this battle. Although she didn't consider Chubby's After Hour Joint to be her "scene," Wilma figured that going out with Shirley would be more entertaining than an early night after tucking in Ronnie, only to fall asleep listening to a Lena Horne record.

"Take Five" by Dave Brubeck played as a mixed crowd of well-dressed people filled the space. Shirley and her husband Jerry danced on the dance floor. Jerry was 35 but moved like he was 25. He was tall and lengthy, giving him what his friends called his "long dancer's legs." He and Shirley were definitely the best dancers in the joint, although they would never admit it. Wilma was not much of a dancer and found more enjoyment leaning against the bar watching Shirley and Jerry ironically "take five."

Lester was a muscular, Negro officer who, still in his uniform, approached the bar. This was a normal occurrence since no one jumped at the sight of such an authority figure. He studied

Wilma from head to toe. Wilma glanced at him staring at her and chose to ignore him. Although Lester filled out his uniform well, Wilma never really found cops attractive. Even if she wasn't doing anything wrong, she tended to feel uncomfortable around them. Most Negroes felt that way, even if the officer was black. For black people it seemed like the term "innocent until proven guilty" was reversed. Lester waved his hand to signal the bartender. Smoothly signaling the attractive woman in front of him was next on his agenda.

"Shot of the Cuddy, Mike," said Lester.

Mike, the bartender, poured the shot as Lester eyes finally caught Wilma's.

"Actually, make it two."

Mike acknowledged the official order and poured out another shot. Lester turned his body to face Wilma.

"You know that's for you," said Lester

"Can't be. I don't drink," retorted Wilma.

"Why are you here?"

"I don't have to drink to enjoy myself."

"Know why I drink Cuddy Shark?"

"Not a clue."

"I'm gonna be the Captain of my ship one day. Show *The Man* that we are as good as any of them."

Lester downed his shot. The psychological significance of his comment was geared more toward how even as a cop, Lester faced discrimination and feelings of inferiority. This sentiment plagued the black community. All Wilma heard was another egocentric man talking about how great he was which prompted her to walk away. Shirley was keeping an eye on Wilma the whole time and decided to bring her in on the fun. She grabbed Wilma and pulled her to the dance floor. Wilma started dancing with Shirley, less enthusiastically, but she valued the escapism from Lester.

The next of Wilma's admirers that night was Jack Norment, a Negro man who matched Wilma in age and height and almost in physical attractiveness. He wore casual clothes, which made him stand out from all of the well-dressed folk dancing and drinking around him. Jack had been with a lot of

women but there was something about Wilma Bailey that drew
him in. He couldn't stop watching her dance. All he had to do
was create the right moment to talk to her. Fate wanted them to
meet because that moment created itself. A patron, who couldn't
hold his liquor, stumbled over to a dancing Wilma and slapped
her ass. Wilma smacked his hand away but he had no intentions
to leave her alone.

Jack finished his drink and walked over to them. Before
the "Ass Slapper" had time to react, Jack grabbed him by the
collar and pulled him in close. The Slapper attempted to punch
Jack in the face, but his reflexes were far too fast for that and
Jack put him in a headlock. The altercation caught the attention
of most of the guests and dancing became less entertaining.
Those who wanted more of a physical confrontation were
disappointed. Jack whispered something in his ear, which visibly
shook the man. Jack, still holding his arm, showed him to the
door. The Ass Slapper left without a problem so whatever Jack
said, did the job. Lester thought about interfering but this was his
time to relax and not have to worry about conflict. It was this

nonchalant attitude that didn't attract Wilma's attention.

Chubby was a 55 year old, overweight, and dark-skinned woman. Her size and her attitude instilled fear in men and women alike. She had a commanding stage presence, especially now since she was holding a baseball bat. The music stopped playing and suddenly everyone's attention was now on the large club owner who looked like she was about to bust someone's head in, or try out for the Tigers. Jack thought he might not get his chance after all.

"Can't y'all remember the motto? Take it outside or wish you died!" said Chubby loudly.

Everyone in the bar was silent and focused their attentions on the swaying bat. There was a rumor going around that a drunken guy called Chubby a "lard ass" which was a trigger for her to beat him to a pulp with a bat before throwing him out of her club. It was apparent that no one there that night wanted to find out if that rumor was true. While the patrons stared at the bat in awe, Chubby took this opportunity to promote her kitchen.

"Don't forget our dinner special; fried catfish and fries.

Remember the kitchen closes at four," said Chubby, more level headedly than before.

The music resumed playing and Chubby walked off the stage. Chubby approached a couple of middle-aged white men in suits and she handed one of them an envelope before they all retreated into the backroom. Shirley and Jerry went back to their "dirty dancing." Wilma checked out Jack and admired his handsomeness. Jack's eyes met with Wilma's. Jack didn't even have to speak first.

"I could have handled that," said Wilma confidently.

"I'm sure," said Jack sarcastically.

Jack extended his hand to shake. Not everyone looked the other person in the eye as they shook hands, but Jack was someone who did. He knew the significance of a handshake was to establish a physical connection with the actual movement of the hands but also connect on an emotional level by making eye contact while doing it.

"Jack," he said.

"Wilma," she said.

"Can I buy you a drink?"

"No. I'm leaving, actually."

Wilma was attracted to Jack. There was no doubt about that. But she hadn't been attracted to a guy in a long time. Sure, she looked upon men who weren't hard on the eyes, but this was the first encounter in awhile that piqued her interest. But because she had not felt these emotions in so long, they felt foreign to her, which made her uncomfortable. Retreating to her "safe zone" with Shirley seemed like the right thing to do in that moment. Wilma left Jack standing there awkwardly and interrupted Shirley's dancing.

"I've had enough excitement for one night," said Wilma.

Shirley looked at Wilma and then at Jack. Jack watched Wilma as he sipped on his drink. He smirked as he swallowed simply because both ladies were checking him out. Shirley smiled and grabbed Wilma's arm, bringing her back to Jack.

"This is Wilma. As the best hair stylist in the Midwest, she expects excellence. What makes you excellent?" inquired Shirley.

She hated Shirley for putting her in awkward situations yet she loved her for having an audacity that Wilma had not yet developed.

"I don't have a ring on my finger," said Jack.

"Uh-huh. Come on Wilma, I want to introduce you to someone," said Shirley bluntly.

Wilma had a decision to make. Was she going to go with Shirley, probably be introduced to another one of her husband's conceited friends, maybe get a kiss, and then go home unsatisfied? Or was she going to give this new guy a chance? A guy who already protected her and expressed interest in her. The choice was clear.

"Where do you work?" asked Wilma.

All Shirley could do was shake her head but as long as Wilma was talking to someone of the opposite sex, she was happy. Shirley drunkenly stumbled back toward Jerry leaving the two new "love birds" to break the ice. Jack and Wilma found seating at a nearby table.

"Chevrolet Gear and Axle. On the assembly line," replied

Jack.

"You make cars?"

"Just the important parts."

"Unfortunately, I work with people. They talk and move while I have scissors in my hands."

Jack coughed on his drink. Getting cut with scissors wasn't the most pleasant thought. He was confused for a moment why Wilma would even mention using scissors but luckily he wasn't too drunk to forget Shirley's contextual comment.

"The best in the Midwest, I've heard."

"Shirley exaggerates but I do want to open my own salon one day."

Jack laughed snidely. Jack came from a very traditional family near Memphis, Tennessee in a little town called; Whitesville. He was raised to believe that it was a man's duty to provide for his family while the woman embraced a more domestic lifestyle. To him, Wilma as a business owner was comedic in the sense that any woman with such responsibility would be dwarfed by what a man could do. He immediately thought of the television personality, Lucy, who portrayed any workingwoman as a parody. Wilma found Jack's laugh to be condescending, which soured her perspective of him.

"What's so funny?" asked Wilma.

Knowing Jack couldn't bash the feminist ideology in the first encounter, needed to think of a good reason for laughing that didn't paint himself as a disrespectful and chauvinist pig. But he did want to question Wilma's "bold" desire. He decided to make his response more relatable by bringing their race into the conversation.

"What Negro woman can make real money doing hair?" asked Jack.

"I guess you've never heard of Madame C. J. Walker."

"No. Who's that?"

"Never mind."

Wilma could not blame Jack for not knowing who her idol was. Not many men were familiar with or even chose to acknowledge the first Negro self-made millionaire in America. In the early 20th century, Walker accumulated her vast wealth by creating and marketing a popular line of beauty and hair products, specifically geared toward Negro women. Wilma would only use her products because they were the best in the industry. At her booth, Wilma hung a photograph of Madam C. J. Walker proudly; secretly hoping one of the clients would recognize her and start up a conversation about such an iconic figure. There was no doubt in Wilma's mind that she too could achieve the fame of Madame C. J. Walker, even if it took her years. Opening her own salon would be the first step.

"Where's your husband?" asked Jack.

"Don't know. Don't care. He ended up becoming an alcoholic."

It was in that moment when a waitress put another drink on the table, in front of Jack.

"Good thing I only drink socially. I wouldn't want to screw up my chances for a second date," said Jack boldly.

"Meaning that this is the first?" asked Wilma in a tone that blended anticipation and skepticism perfectly.

"You're having fun aren't you?"

If Wilma learned anything relevant about Jack that night was that he was confident. He stood up to an unruly drunk and talked to her with a conviction that was mysterious and enticing. The answer to Jack's rhetorical question was yes. Wilma was having fun. For the first time in years, she was falling in love.

Chapter 5: 1956-1957

New Years Eve, 1956 was a night like any of the other last days of the year. It was a night of reflection. America "liked Ike" enough to give him a second term. Part of it had to do with Eisenhower signing the Federal Aid Highway Act, which would eventually give all the cars coming out of Detroit more room to "stretch their legs." Since Henry Ford's Model T and the first American freeway construction, Detroit had been dubbed "The Motor City" and the economy was flourishing. The Dow Jones Industrial Average closed above 500 for the first time, which had less to do with Eisenhower's leadership, and more to do with Detroit making cars for the whole country and accumulating the money for the stock market to manage.

Eisenhower's popularity and moral conviction lead him to sign a Joint Resolution of Congress to authorize "In God We Trust" as the U.S. national motto. This motto would serve as a powerful lesson to Wilma later in her life. Beyond New Years Eve being a night of introspection, it was also a night to look to the future. For Wilma Bailey, her future arrived in the form of a second son.

"Oh, my God!" Wilma shrieked.

As a God fearing woman, Wilma yelled the Lord's name to give her strength in the hospital room that night.

"Push! Push! Almost there, Wilma!" said Doctor Price firmly.

Wilma grasped the silver handle on the side of the bed tightly. The diamond ring she wore reflected the tinsel that hung from the ceiling. For Wilma, focusing on the decorations distracted her from the severe pain she was feeling. Doctor Price was a middle-aged white man who was accompanied by Nurse Angela, a younger white nurse. She stood silent behind Doctor Price has he crouched in front of a propped up Wilma. It was Nurse Angela's first birthing and her shocked face emulated that. This was not the most settling thing to gaze upon while giving birth, Wilma's eyes darted back up to the tinsel and her screams ripped through the entire hospital.

In the hallway outside the room, sat Jack. He wore a sweat-stained suit and was shaking his legs anxiously as Wilma's excruciating cries penetrated his eardrums. One hand played with his gold ring band on the other. Since his legs were already shaking uncontrollably, Jack decided he might as well move around. He began pacing back and forth when he made eye contact with the elderly receptionist seated at a nearby desk. Jack approached her. The woman displayed a look of discomfort that many people her age would give Negro men. As Jack leaned towards the counter, the receptionist slid her chair back more.

"Do we still win if the baby is born a few minutes early?" asked Jack.

"I'm sorry, it's hospital rules. It has to be the first baby born in the New Year," said the receptionist timidly.

The receptionist's soft-spoken response was barely heard since Wilma had just expelled her loudest scream. Jack ran for the first time in months. He was excited to see his firstborn child, secretly hoping it was a boy and that a certain contest was won.

Jack barged into the room and was surprised not to see the baby right away. Jack tracked the origin of the baby's wailing to Nurse Angela, who was cleaning the baby with her back facing them. Jack ran next to Wilma and crouched beside her bed. Wilma managed to smile at Jack in between her deep gasps for air. Doctor Price was cleaning himself off when Jack felt the need to open his big mouth.

"Well, Doc...Did we win?"

Wilma squinted her eyes at Jack as her panting subsided. Doctor Price looked up at the clock on the wall and then at Jack.

"No. It's 11:57 and you shouldn't even be in here."

Jack looked at his silver watch that had a shininess matching Wilma's diamond ring.

"Mine says midnight and I'm not leaving my wife's side."

"Jack, drop it," said Wilma as she exhaled.

"We can always use the money, baby," said Jack.

"We can claim him for the whole year. Drop it," declared Wilma.

Jack always had a short fuse and was close to saying something snarky but unlike his first question earlier, this time he luckily thought before he spoke. He diffused his anger internally and gave the weary mother of his newborn child a break.

"You're right, baby. That will be just fine."

Nurse Angela slowly walked toward the new parents, holding the baby, wrapped in a blue blanket. Wilma's eyes lit up, conveying a euphoric expression that Jack had never seen before.

"Say hello to your new son," said Nurse Angela delightfully.

Jack sighed subtly with relief but just enough for Wilma to notice and give him a glare that was equally as subtle. Nurse Angela slowly lowered the baby into Wilma's arms.

"He's beautiful!" said Wilma.

"And ready to come out. His eyes were wide open," said Nurse Angela.

Wilma and Jack gazed lovingly at their child.

In 1957, Joanne was 30 years old. Any observer would deem Joanne and Wilma sisters from their similar bone structures and complexions. Wilma and Joanne were more than just sisters. They were best friends, unbeknownst to Shirley. Wilma and Joanne became each other's confidants and Wilma used to always practice doing Joanne's hair growing up. Because of their father's alcoholism, Bunny alienated herself from her family and eventually found refuge in the Navy of all places. Bunny was a family member who would only show up for Christmas or a funeral whereas Joanne was just a phone call away. It was especially convenient that Joanne moved to Detroit as well. She became the "go to babysitter" for Ronnie when Wilma needed rest or her and Jack insisted on alone time.

Joanne babysat Ronnie during the delivery, which was a loving thing to do considering all the parties she missed out on. She held Ronnie's hand tightly when they entered the hospital that early morning of the newly arrived 1957. Joanne picked him up and gave him a piggyback ride to the hospital room.

"Oh Wilma, Jack, he's precious," said Joanne glowingly.

It was one o'clock in the morning but everyone was wide-awake, except for the baby. Wilma rocked him slowly as Joanne gawked over him. Ronnie stood by the door and pouted because he wasn't getting all of the attention but he also wanted to have a sister like his friend down the street, as if having a sister made one cool. But like living with his physical condition, he would adapt and learn.

"Ronnie, come meet your baby brother," said Wilma.

Ronnie began his slow trek across the room and hesitantly inched toward the bed. Ronnie gazed upon his new sibling with a sense of wonder.

"What did you name him?" inquired Joanne.

"I wanted to name him Jack Junior..." chimed in Jack.

"His name is Frederick," said Wilma."

Joanne gave a nod of approval after hearing the name. During their youth, Wilma and Joanne were taught of Frederick Douglass' legacy. Wilma thought that naming her son after such an influential social reformer would be a way to honor the tenacity that Douglass embodied. In an uncertain world, Wilma wanted her son to have that same perseverance.

"Well, at least he's got your last name, Jack," joked Joanne.

The Norment/Bailey family grew by one more on that New Years morning. Their time of reflection had turned into an appreciation for the current moment. Wilma and Jack watched the sunrise from the hospital window that morning. The sun glowed with optimism; hope for the future. The country they lived in might not have been perfect, but their family was.

"I'm taking this off," said Wilma.

"Just wait until I park," replied Jack.

Wilma was blindfolded and sat in the passenger seat of Jack's white Chevrolet Impala. Snow flurries fell gracefully on this cold January day, which caused Jack to drive a little slower. Jack was grinning like a young schoolboy who just won a spelling bee. He was excited to show Wilma something that would benefit their family tremendously.

"Jack, this surprise better not be another electric mixer," said Wilma.

Wilma was half kidding when she uttered that statement. Last time Jack surprised her with something, it was a new household item that did not particularly make Wilma "jump for joy" even if it did harness the wonder of electricity. In her heart, she could tell that right now Jack's excitement for this surprise far outweighed the enthusiasm he had when he gifted Wilma with the mixer. The car stopped and Jack got out and opened Wilma's door to let her out. Jack removed the blindfold and exposed Wilma to a two story, red brick house with large windows and a spacious front porch. Wilma was in awe of the beauty of this west side home. Wilma couldn't believe someone as frugal as Jack would pay for such a luxurious house, which prompted her inquiry.

"Whose house is this?"

"Ours. I'm sick of that cramped apartment."

"How did we afford this?"

"I took some money out of your account."

Wilma's face dropped. She was dumbfounded at Jack's decision. For a man who tended to bash women who worked and promote the ideology that men should pay for everything, this comment seemed out of character. But when it came to living comfortably, Jack would break his rigid rules from time to time. In this case, Jack wanted to have more space to raise a family and an apartment was not conducive to that.

"Don't you want a nice place to raise our son? We

deserve it, baby," said Jack.

Wilma loved the house but hated Jack's deception, and it was that duplicity that distorted her vision of the house.

"It doesn't have to be this big," said Wilma decisively.

"Come here," commanded Jack.

Jack grabbed Wilma's arm and led her to the large backyard, which had two large apple trees.

"Don't you want the kids playing in this huge yard?"

Wilma silently admired the yard as she envisioned her two sons growing up together, climbing the trees to fetch apples for her to make future pies. She wasn't ready to admit that to Jack though. He needed to show her more in order to build up her satisfaction to his level.

"Wait 'till you see the inside," declared Jack.

Jack excitedly led the way. It was like he was a kid in a candy shop whose source of sugar came from house itself. He opened the back door and let Wilma in. They entered the kitchen, which had wooden cabinets, and a new refrigerator appliance.

"You've got so much cooking space," said Jack.

"Yeah, I bet you miss the meals since my pregnancy."

"But baby, you know I don't mind cooking."

"Yeah, you're right, it's a nice kitchen," said Wilma in a conceding tone.

Jack proceeded to run down a hallway. Wilma slowly followed. She entered the master bedroom. Jack jumped out at Wilma from the side, pushed her up against a wall, and kissed her passionately. Wilma knew in that moment that Jack was using his sexual prowess to help sell the house but knowing that didn't stop from turning her on. They conversed in between kisses.

"If anything should sway you, it should be the size of this bedroom," said Jack.

"Jack, we can't leave the kids at Joanne's all day."

"Come on, baby. Can we keep it? Do it for the kids."

Jack's sales pitch utilized pathos once again by bringing the argument back to making a better life for the children. Sure Jack spent a lot of money, money from working at Doris' that was supposed to go for a nest egg for her new shop, but she gave into Jack anyway for the notion of raising a family in a single family home; the American Dream.

"That backyard is pretty big. It kind of reminds me of home," said Wilma warmly.

"That's my baby," responded Jack.

Jack started kissing her neck. Wilma bit her lower lip and was clearly into it.

"Jack, stop playing," said Wilma.

As turned on as she was, she did not want to risk the health and condition of her body by having intercourse so shortly after giving birth. Wilma would never look at Jack the same way knowing what he was capable of such financial deceit, but her nest egg paid off and now she would be living the "good life" in a big home on the Westside of Detroit.

Chapter 6: Spring 1959

In the last two years, Civil Rights continued its turbulent journey with triumphs and setbacks. A few weeks after Frederick's birth, a 24-year-old Negro truck driver, Willie Edwards, was beaten by Ku Klux Klan members and was forced to jump off of a bridge in Alabama. Edwards died and his body was not discovered for another three months. When the Edwards killing was broadcasted on the radio, Jack kept reiterating to his family how fortunate they were to be living in a city that did not cater to the Jim Crow Laws that plagued the south.

In the spring of 1959, however, Wilma was coming to terms with the fact that the "good life" she envisioned when her family moved to the Westside, was not what she thought it would be. It was a lifestyle bound to the home without a working job to keep her busy. Much to Wilma's discontent, Jack insisted that Wilma stay home to take care of the kids while he worked at Chevrolet Gear & Axle to "bring home the bacon." Jack was much more traditional in his mindset, but what frustrated Wilma was that the family would have more money if he was the one who would stay at home. Jack only made two dollars an hour while Wilma could easily make fifty dollars in a day by only having to do a few clients' hair or setting a few wigs. The idea of a woman working and a man taking care of the kids was a taboo topic at that time and Wilma didn't want to start any waves in that ocean. Besides, sailing along with her children did give Wilma a certain level of fulfillment even if it wasn't the occupational kind she had been used to.

In 1959, Ronnie was seven years old and went through his own version of "discontentment." Because of his disfigured face, he was not the most approachable kid and did not have many friends because of it. He found refuge in the school's science room in which there was a tank filled with many sea creatures. He would admire the small lizards and iguanas, sometimes talking to them.

One day that spring, Ronnie approached the glass wall of the aquarium and stared at a green colored chameleon, which was sitting on a log away from the other lizards. Ronnie related to the creature and projected his own loneliness onto it.

"Don't worry, I'll be your friend," said Ronnie softly.

Ronnie looked around the room to make sure that it was empty before he slowly reached his hand into the biosphere. Ronnie grabbed the chameleon and put it in his backpack. He left the science room with one of the biggest smiles he had in months.

Unbeknownst to his family during his elementary years, Ronnie would "borrow" many animals from Brady Elementary to take care of them and watch them roam freely around his room. The science teacher did not care about animals as much as Ronnie and never noticed the missing creatures. Unlike his peers, the animals did not judge Ronnie. The animals did not call him "crooked face" or laugh at him. Whenever asked what he wanted to be when he grew up, Ronnie responded with: "a Veterinarian." Although Ronnie did not have the strongest social skills or charming good looks, he had a pure heart and treated all of his animals with gentleness and kindness.

While Ronnie was at school, Wilma would take care Frederick who she nick named; "Ricky" When the baby slept, she found herself doing house chores, and making sure dinner was cooked and ready for a hungry Jack. It was not all monotonous. She would have to change up the house chores. Vacuum one day, dust the next, and dedicate an entire day to laundry. Maintaining a larger house was a lot of work. The thought that kept her going was making sure Ronnie and Ricky were taken care of. She could have tried to convince Jack for her to go back to work and recruit a babysitter for the boys, but she did not. She loved her sons too much and enjoyed spending time with them. Whether it was consoling a sad Ronnie or being with Ricky during his pivotal moments of growth, Wilma loved being a mother.

She clapped Ricky on encouragingly as he took his first steps that spring. Experiencing that moment made all the house chores that month, worth it. Wilma did know that as Ricky grew, he would not need his mother as much. It was a rainy day in Detroit. "Am I Blue" by Billie Holiday played on the radio in Wilma's bedroom, which matched the tone of the weather outside. Wilma was cleaning out her closet when she stumbled upon her old vinyl styling bag. She dusted it off and gave a nostalgic grin. She missed Doris' and she missed doing hair. She decided then and there that she would go back to doing what she loved no matter what Jack said. It was all about timing.

At the Chevrolet Gear & Axle Plant, Jack necessarily was not doing what he loved but what he needed to do. Loud mechanical noises filled the giant place of car creation. He and five other workers (two black and three white) assembled wheel axles on the assembly line. Their uniforms were stained with sweat, tar, and grease. Jack had a few friends on the line but focused his attention more on his job than any social situation, making him one of the hardest workers in the plant. Mr. Jones was a middle-aged white man and a corporate "higher upper" of the company. He made his rounds on the assembly line to assess the productivity of the day. He usually had minimal interactions with the workers and kept his opinions to himself. His attention was narrowly focused on his clipboard that he wrote diligently on. One day in April 1959, Mr. Jones came to the line without a clipboard. This threw off a lot of the workers. Mr. Jones approached Jack personally.

"The boss wants to see you," said Mr. Jones flatly.

The black and white workers around him looked at Mr. Jones and Jack with curiosity and confusion. Jack asked the question that everyone on the assembly line was thinking about asking.

"What for?"

"We're about to find out. Let's go," said Mr. Jones.

Mr. Jones walked passed Jack, expecting him to follow. Jack did just that. After spending a few seconds studying the back of Mr. Jones' balding head, he looked around him to see workers staring at him smugly and disdainfully. He made eye contact with an older worker.

"Jack, you not brownnosing the boss, is you?"

Jack had to keep following a swift moving Jones, leaving any conversation as an impossibility. All Jack could do was shrug his shoulders and keep on walking.

Mr. Schnaar was a middle-aged white man who had achieved a lot in his life before becoming the Superintendent of GM. He sat at his desk which was cluttered with paperwork and small model cars. He sipped on his coffee between writing.

Different mechanical parts of a car decorated his office shelves. A framed one-dollar bill hung on the wall behind him. After knocking, Mr. Jones and Jack entered the office. Mr. Jones sat down on the right side of the room while Jack stood awkwardly by a seat that was positioned in front of Mr. Schnaar's desk.

"Take a seat, Jack," said Mr. Schnaar.

Jack studied the room and took his seat slowly. He then turned and looked at Mr. Jones, who was staring at him. Before Jack could turn his head back to face Mr. Schnaar, the reason Jack was summoned was revealed.

"I'm promoting you to Foreman," said Mr. Schnaar.

Mr. Jones was clearly surprised but chose not to say anything. Jack tried to hold back his excitement, but his smile became too strong to contain. Mr. Schnaar signaled to Mr. Jones.

"Jones will walk you through all of your duties today and tomorrow. You'll start Monday."

"What's the catch?" asked Jack.

"No catch," responded Mr. Schnaar.

"All those white employees out there, why me?"

Mr. Schnaar didn't want this conversation to go into race. All he wanted to do was be cordial and convince Jack that this promotion was solely based on his work ethic, but Jack's pressing nature made Mr. Schnaar delve deeper.

"The Union says we need some more black foremen. You come to work everyday. Why not you?"

"Oh yeah?" questioned Jack with a tinge of sarcasm.

"Yeah. You want it or not?"

The answer was obvious.

On the same day, Wilma played with two-year-old Ricky on the living room floor. She rolled a small ball to him and he held onto it tightly. There was a knock on the front door and Wilma got up to answer it. It was someone she hadn't talked to in months; a friend Wilma thought forgot about her. But who could forget the talented Wilma Bailey? Shirley sure as hell couldn't. After exchanging pleasantries, Shirley conveyed her feelings.

"I miss you at the salon, Wilma,"

"I know. I miss it too. Once Ricky starts school, I hope to go back."

"Great. You see how my hair looks? The new girl means well, but no one can do my hair like you," said Shirley genuinely.

Wilma hadn't smiled like that since Ricky learned how to walk. There was an awkward silence, which had never happened before with Shirley. Wilma chalked it up to all the time apart, which limited familiarity. The spouse question seemed like a good segue.

"How's Jerry?"

"Boring as ever. But, hey, me and some of my girlfriends are going to Chubby's tonight. You have to come."

Wilma lit up for a second. The thought of going out excited Wilma, especially since she only spent time with Shirley occasionally ever since Ricky was born. Just as she was about to say yes, she remembered a certain ritual.

"I can't. Fridays are usually our...*night*."

"Make it up to him later. We haven't been out in ages!"

"I don't know, Shirley. With Ricky..."

"I have a surprise for you," said Shirley mysteriously.

Last time Wilma was surprised she got a house that she

unknowingly paid for. She was a bit jaded in the "surprise" department, but Shirley had always been a good friend. Wilma knew that whatever surprise Shirley had up her sleeve, it was probably something worthwhile. Wilma smiled at Shirley, which was all the confirmation both of them needed.

That same night, Jack rode the city bus from work to home. Although he was originally regretting letting Wilma borrow the car for the day, any negative feelings were gone now that he got his promotion. Jack was always good at hiding his emotions but during that bus ride he looked out the window and smiled. Edna was a 33 year old, dark-skinned black woman, wearing nurse clothing, who sat a few seats behind Jack and to the left. She noted his smile.

"I always see you on this bus and you've never smiled once," said Edna.

Jack looked back and gazed upon the attractive woman. He was taken aback by her glowing smile and long black hair. Seeing Edna's hair reminded him of how he wished Wilma wore longer hair. They were the only two passengers on board.

"I got promoted today," said Jack proudly.

"That's something to smile about," said Edna.

"You're telling me."

"Oh, you big time now, huh?" asked Edna playfully.

Jack laughed.

"Not yet," he replied.

Edna gazed at his wedding band. Her smile faded for a second.

"Your wife must be so proud of you," said Edna.

"She will be," said Jack with hesitance in his voice.

Saved by the stop. The bus came to a halt and Edna stood up to leave. She walked down the bus and handed Jack a piece of paper. Jack took it and watched Edna walk off the bus. Jack opened the folded note. It read:

"Edna: 555-5333"

Jack smiled and put the note in his pocket. For Jack, the day just kept getting better and better.

Back at home, Wilma wore a black dress and quickly set the kitchen table while listening to "Stormy Weather" by her favorite artist, Lena Horne on the radio. Ricky followed under his mother's feet, which forced Wilma to slow down her movements. On the floor in the living room was Ronnie playing with his green army men toys. Playing with his new pet lizard, Godzilla would be his private evening activity. Jack entered the house.

"Honey, I'm home."

Jack mimicked a character from a show he despised. This confused Wilma during her walk toward him, but at least his tone was pleasant. It might make what she was about to say less of a problem. She kissed and hugged him.

"I made your favorite dish, baby," said Wilma

"Smells good and damn you look fine," said Jack as he checked out his wife.

"Thank you."

Wilma led him into the kitchen but Jack stopped in his tracks.

"Wilma," said Jack in a serious voice.

Wilma looked at him inquisitively. Maybe it would be harder to tell him her evening plans after all.

"I got promoted!" said Jack zealously.

"Wow. That's great baby."

She hugged him again. He expected her to be more excited and maybe he would have received a passionate kiss. But all he got was a half-ass affirmation with a hug that was only slightly tighter than the first one. She let go and walked toward the kitchen. Jack ignored Ronnie on the floor and went straight to picking up Ricky.

"You hear that Ricky! Your Daddy is gonna be a Foreman!"

Ronnie stared sadly at them for a second then went back to playing with his army men. Wilma sat down at the table and looked at the clock above the counter. Her body language conveyed that she wanted to "get this show on the road" by starting dinner. Jack placed Ricky in his high chair and sat down himself.

"Get over here, Ronnie," said Jack sternly.

Ronnie stood up and ran over to take his seat at the table, fearing what Jack might do if he wasn't as fast as he should be.

"Keep playing with those army men and I'm gonna enlist you myself," said Jack jokingly.

Ronnie started eating his chicken silently.

"Foreman. What does that mean exactly?" asked Wilma.

"Instead of being on the line, I will be in charge of scheduling the line, and making sure all the workers do their jobs right."

Jack stuffed a large piece of chicken in his mouth and kept talking as he chewed.

"Even the white ones."

"So I take it you didn't tell Mr. Schnaar to go to hell for making you work late last week?" inquired Wilma sarcastically.

"The workers will crucify him for promoting me, but I'm gonna enjoy this while it lasts."

Ricky smudged food all over his face and Wilma cleaned him up. The sound of a loud car horn was heard right outside the house. Wilma stood up abruptly and walked to the living room. She looked out the window and saw that Shirley was behind the wheel of red 1958 Cadillac. Wilma fetched her coat from the closet.

"Where are you going?" asked Jack interrogatively.

"I meant to tell you this sooner, but Shirley asked me to go out with her tonight."

Jack got up and walked toward Wilma. He changed his tone to be friendlier.

"Baby, it's Friday! And I want to celebrate my promotion!"

Jack grabbed her hands and motioned his head toward the bedroom.

"Maybe tomorrow night. I haven't seen Shirley in months."

Jack stared coldly at Wilma. He let go of her hands and shook his head, dismissively. He went back to sit down and finish his chicken.

"Put the kids to bed by nine, okay?"

Jack acknowledged her with a quick nod as he chewed. Wilma left and the sound of the door shutting seemed louder than normal. Jack threw his fork down, with less of an appetite than he had earlier. Jack went to the bedroom to change out of his work clothes. He pulled out Edna's note from his pocket. He studied the number and then looked the rotary phone on the dresser. He contemplated doing what he thought any red-blooded man would do, but that thought vanished when Ricky started crying from the kitchen. Tonight he would continue his job as a supportive father.

Chubby's After Hour Joint was decently crowded with a giant smoke cloud hovering over the patrons. Wilma, Shirley, and her friends sat at the bar. Wilma felt left out due to Shirley and her friends shooting off inside jokes about experiences with men. Wilma listened politely and forced a laugh when it was socially appropriate. Part of her was regretting not celebrating her *night* at home.

Did Shirley make up that there was a surprise to get me to come out? thought Wilma.

Two men in gray Continental style suits entered the joint and opened the doors for Mr. Silverman, a white man in his late 40s, with a receding hairline. He wore a black and white suit. He stomped on his cigarette before entering. Shirley glanced at the men and signaled them over to the bar. Mr. Silverman walked over with the two men following behind. They stopped behind Wilma.

"Wilma, I want to introduce you to a friend of mine; Mr. Silverman."

Wilma turned to face him. She extended her hand. Mr. Silverman was impressed with her initiative and shook her hand slowly while smiling at her. Mr. Silverman sat with the ladies but the other two men stood behind him and surveyed the establishment. They were clearly bodyguards, which made Wilma perceive her new acquaintance as a man of importance.

"I've heard a lot about you, Miss Bailey," Mr. Silverman said in a deep voice.

Mr. Silverman had distinctive eyebrows that added an underlying seriousness to his outward charm.

"Please, call me Wilma. Everyone does."

"Shirley speaks very highly of your cosmetic talents."

Wilma looked over at Shirley and started to blush.

"I've always loved doing hair," she said nonchalantly.

"She tells me that you want to open your own shop."

"Not anytime soon. I just bought a house on the Westside."

"Well, I wanted to tell you that there is a space available on Linwood and Glendale," said Mr. Silverman in an opportunistic tone.

Wilma's instant sense of optimism regarding such a business venture came as quickly as it and went.

"If I had the money," said Wilma regretfully.

"I could help you out. Shirley is a friend of mine, and she says you're hard working and reliable."

Was this the surprise Shirley spoke of? My dream handed to me on a silver platter from some debonair guy named Silverman? Too good to be true, right? thought Wilma.

"That is very nice of you, but I couldn't," uttered Wilma.

Mr. Silverman's eyes focused on Shirley almost as if it was a signal for her to chime in.

"Wilma, Mr. Silverman helped Jerry and I get started. He's a good man."

Wilma looked over at the spot where she met Jack four years earlier. Her thoughts raced to that moment when Jack laughed and scoffed at the idea of Wilma opening her own salon. She then analyzed how much of her drive and passion had subsided since she married Jack. She always wanted children, there was no doubt about that. But she never intended to be a housewife. Wilma saw this as the chance of a lifetime yet she hated being indebted to others. Wilma then thought that she didn't need any handouts but could go back to Doris' again and save money for her own salon. Wilma looked at Shirley, a woman who was always well-dressed and had a confidence that no one could shake. If Mr. Silverman had helped Shirley to be where she is now, then this offer seemed legitimate. If her salon was a successful business like she knew it would be, paying back this Mr. Silverman for the initial investment would not take long at all. Wilma began shaking her legs with nervousness and excitement. She looked into Shirley's eyes and then Mr. Silverman's.

They were serious. This was serious, thought Wilma.

"What do you want to do, Wilma?" asked Mr. Silverman.

Wilma smiled.

"I know what that means!" said Shirley with an upward inflection.

Finally, Wilma Bailey was going to open her own salon.

Chapter 7: Summer 1959

It only took a few months to transform the empty building on Linwood and Glendale to the spacious and lavish salon called "Bailey's." It was the summer of 1959 and a sunny day in Detroit. Wilma stood in front of a large window that had been freshly painted with "Bailey's Salon" in bright red letters. She held her favorite pair of scissors and hovered over a long red ribbon that hung in front of the entrance doors. Shirley and a dozen other women, who knew Wilma from Doris', circled around Wilma and cheered her on. Wilma cut the ribbon slowly and the ribbon fell gracefully onto the ground as the cheering reached a higher decibel level. Wilma could not contain her smile. The dream that she had since she first started styling hair, came true that day.

She now had her own salon. Now she could make her own schedule, use her favorite products, emphasize quality and attention to detail as opposed to quantity of clients and incompetent work that was far too common in the many salons she worked at. Although she may not reach Madame C. J. Walker status, she was the first woman in her family to own a business and that in itself was something she took pride in.

Wilma's first day was upbeat and busy. Shirley was in charge of "getting the word out" about Bailey's and that word went everywhere. The salon was packed with women from all over Detroit, excited to beautify themselves. On the jukebox played "What'd I Say" by Ray Charles. One lyric Wilma really enjoyed from that song was: "Baby, it's all right, baby, it's all right now." This idea became sort of a mantra for Wilma and a defense mechanism against conflict. But there were minimal conflicts on opening day.

Wilma's colorful new staff had rigorous training the week before and implemented Wilma's policies flawlessly. Anita and Janette, looking younger than their 1963 counterparts, styled while bobbing their heads to Ray Charles. A younger Kathy focused all her attention on Wilma styling Shirley's hair. Kathy would need more training before Wilma felt comfortable giving her a client. A younger Moe, stacked fresh white towels on the back shelf and walked out without saying anything. All the linen was washed and dried at Silverman's Cleaners, which was the business that Mr. Silverman managed. Moe's towel delivery would become a weekly service and a testament to how lucrative this business venture was for Wilma. She had financial support like never before from someone who recognized her talents and believed in her.

Ronnie, at age five, held his two year old brother Ricky as they spun in one of the salon chairs happily. As the day died down, Wilma decided to give Kathy her first cosmetic job. She allowed Kathy to put a blonde streak right through the middle of Wilma' black hair. Wilma studied herself in the mirror and wondered if Jack would like her new hairstyle. Jack was supposed to come and help her open but he never did. He was against the salon from the beginning so it was no surprise that he did not show up, but Wilma still had a smidgen of hope. The blonde streak represented her independence. She could style her hair anyway she wanted. She was in control of her own life and she would no longer let anyone tell her what to do.

Instead of supporting his wife, Jack sat at a table in

Detroit's Green Leaf Restaurant. Across the table, sat the woman he met on the bus: Edna. Edna wore a tight red dress that punctuated her curves in an enticing way. Jack was not the best conversationalist that night. His attention was focused more on Edna's appearance. Any story or comment mentioned about her work in the hospital was acknowledged with a "mhm" or a grunt that translated to pretending to care. One tidbit that Jack processed was that Edna was divorced and had one son and two daughters. Edna's mind also wandered during the meal as she admired Jack's arm muscles, formed from such strenuous assembly line activity. An attraction between them was undeniable and both of them did not want their nights to end in a delicatessen. When Edna mentioned that her children were gone for the night, Jack knew that he was at a crossroads. He had an internal struggle with his own demons in that moment.

You've already pushed this too far. Go to Wilma. See her new shop, thought his metaphorical angel.

She's sexy and she wants you. Don't let this opportunity slip through your fingers, thought his metaphorical devil.

Jack was an opportunist and that night he capitalized on an opportunity that would betray his morality and his family.

A Hollywood style spotlight illuminated the clouds outside of Bailey's. The shop was now empty after a successful opening day. In the backroom of the salon, Wilma counted her first day's earnings. Content with the final amount, she put the cash into a safe hidden within a cabinet. Wilma came out of the backroom and gazed lovingly at Ronnie and Ricky who slept next to each other on the one couch in the salon. Mr. Silverman walked through the front door. This startled Wilma until she realized who it was. Mr. Silverman took note of the sleeping children and approached Wilma quietly.

"I like that streak," said Mr. Silverman genuinely.

Wilma smiled.

"I don't know how to thank you for all your help," said Wilma.

"We'll work out something. Oh, about that jukebox..."

"Oh, yeah. What's the lease on that?"

"Don't worry about it. Just mark your quarters with nail

polish whenever you want to play a song."

"Why?" asked Wilma, confusedly.

"So when we collect our money every week, we'll give you your quarters back."

For someone who owned a commercial laundry, this Silverman was a sly cat, thought Wilma.

"Um. Okay. Thanks," said Wilma.

Mr. Silverman looked down at Ronnie and Ricky sleeping. Like any objective observer, Mr. Silverman's eyes darted straight to Ronnie's chin.

"What happened to your son?"

"He was born with a condition. The doctor recommended the surgery. It didn't heal right."

"Surgery for what?"

"Trachea blockage. He had problems breathing while he was asleep."

"Did they fix that at least?"

"Yeah. But they severed a nerve in the process."

"Did you file for malpractice?"

"When I realized his chin didn't grow, the statute of limitations ran out."

"I'm sorry."

Wilma appreciated Mr. Silverman's concern but she hated pity parties, especially when they reminded her of past traumas. Changing the subject was crucial for her in that moment.

"When do I need to start paying you back?"

"Don't worry, Wilma. I'm gonna work with you."

Wilma took this comment literally and thought it would be a good moment to flex her comedic muscles, that weren't always her strongest.

"A balding white man working here might scare people away," said Wilma jokingly.

Mr. Silverman didn't laugh like Wilma wanted, but she did manage to unearth a smile out of his serious self. Now it was Mr. Silverman's turn to change the subject.

"How much do you know about policy?"

"Policy? What's that?" asked Wilma curiously.

"You know. The numbers," said Mr. Silverman flatly.

Wilma nodded skeptically, understanding "the policy" that Mr. Silverman referred to, yet she did not fathom how this illegal process would involve her. Mr. Silverman explained how he wanted Bailey's to be the epicenter of policy, entailing people coming in and out to bet on the horse races at Hazel Park. Wilma's cut of the profits would be substantial and the more exposure to the shop would attract more business. As Mr. Silverman conveyed all of this, Wilma had an empty feeling in her stomach. As someone who obeyed the laws of the land all her life, she felt uncomfortable allowing something illegal to happen in her salon but how could she say no? She knew that if she wanted to keep her dream alive she had to play ball with this man. She had to trust him.

Chapter 8: Fall 1959

A few months had passed since Bailey's famous debut. Red and orange leaves fell outside Bailey's bustling salon. It was busy not just for the clients, but because of Mr. Silverman's "policy" was now implemented and in full swing. White and black folk alike came in to tell Wilma their three number combinations designating the specific horses that they thought would win that day. It was like the shop had its own language with different numerical combinations being spewed out like the Stock Market.

Each player would play three numbers that represented three horses. The term "win, place, and show," was a common term uttered in that salon that signified which horses took first/win, second/place, and third/show for the last race of the evening at Hazel Park Racetrack. That three number combination dictated the winners of the day. Once Wilma recorded all of the player's numbers, she would read her ledger to Mr. Silverman who would record all of the amounts. Afterwards, she would call Hazel Park and find out the winning numbers and distribute the money at the shop. It was a lucrative market with winnings going into the thousands. It took Wilma a few weeks to be comfortable with this process, but like doing hair, she became an expert.

As Wilma organized supplies in the backroom, her receptionist recorded numbers from the front counter. Janette, Anita, and the newly hired, Bryce, each styled the hair of their respective black women clients. Bryce was finishing up with Marva, a middle-aged, dark-skinned black woman who had a fuse as short as Bryce's. They did not complement each other so well.

"Excuse me?" said Marva incredulously.

"He didn't mean..." interjected Anita, who stood nearby.

"Actually, I did," declared Bryce squeakily.

"Say it to my face then, bean pole," said Marva.

Bryce was used to being called a fag or homo but when anyone would insult him about his body, that would set him off like a firecracker.

"Miss Thing got me started now," yelled Bryce.

Everyone in the shop turned to listen to a boisterous

Bryce.

"All I'm saying is that at this establishment, tipping is encouraged," said Bryce.

Marva stood up, ripped off her apron, and threw it on the floor. Wilma exited the backroom at the right time, assed the situation, and walked over to Marva.

"I'm sorry about that. Next time I'll take care of you for free," said Wilma.

Bryce watched them with his arms folded as he leaned on one leg. Everyone else stared curiously and anxiously waited for what would happen next.

"As long as he's here, I'll never come back," said Marva.

Wilma gave an angry look to Bryce. It was a look that made her question why she hired him in the first place. Marva walked out but before exiting she turned back toward everyone in the salon.

"Didn't think y'all well-to-do colored folks were looking to take every penny. Well, here!" yelled Marva.

Marva emptied her pockets and threw loose change on the

floor right in front of the entrance. Marva slammed the door, which almost knocked over the entrance bell fastened above. Wilma wished Ricky were there in that moment. Much like he would do after a dance, Ricky would be quick to pick up all of the change on the floor of the salon. Wilma turned her attention to Bryce.

"Treat a client like that again and you're gone."

"Wilma, you know she don't tip," said Bryce.

"Maybe it's because her ends are never straight," said Wilma.

Wilma picked up Marva's apron and walked into the backroom. Kim was sitting at her workstation curling a wig. Next to her was a pile of various colored wigs. Wilma placed the apron in a dish tub on the counter and greeted Kim. Kim ignored Wilma and focused all her attention on curling. Kim didn't have the best social skills, but Wilma felt guilty sometimes for leaving her back there all alone.

"You know, you can come out once in awhile," said Wilma.

Kim did not flinch and a few seconds passed before she uttered a response.

"No. No. I no like Bryce."

Wilma laughed. It was the first time she laughed in a long time. Wilma then tried to remember when was the last time she laughed that hard. After a few seconds of sifting through her memories, she remembered that she would always laugh around family. She grew up with a colorful cast of characters with their own quirks. It was in that moment that Wilma got excited to go home for the holidays.

Chapter 9: Winter 1959

It was Christmas at "The Big House." Ricky and Ronnie did not enjoy their time at their grandfather's. The adult conversations bore them, but they were always on their best behavior in front of a disciplinary Jack. Inside the large Victorian house in Grass Lake, Michigan was a lavish family gathering around a long wooden table. A chandelier shone from above, making the shiny china on the table glisten. A Christmas tree stood tall in the corner of the room with presents nestled snugly underneath. Every seat at the table was filled with Wilma's family members.

Harry sat at the head of one side of the table, like any stoic patriarch would. He was a burly and unshaven man. Sitting next to Harry was Wilma's stepmother, Claireece. It took a few years for Wilma and the rest of the siblings to warm up to Claireece. No one would ever be a substitute for their loving mother and it was sometimes hard to gauge how genuine and caring Claireece was. If anything made Wilma more accepting of Claireece, it was her culinary skills and how perfectly the table was set. She obviously cared enough to make this Christmas dinner special.

Next to Claireece, on the left side of the table sat Joanne, Wilma, Ricky, and Ronnie. Jack sat across from Harry on the other end of the table. Jack had an expression on his face that revealed that he did not want to be there. Unbeknownst to the whole family, Jack had been having an affair with Edna for five months and much of his thoughts went to her. Wilma was not ignorant of Jack's detached behavior, but he made her believe it was because of the job stress.

To the left of Jack, on the other side of the table, sat a younger John L. in a bright green sweater. This was John L.'s first Christmas in a long time and he looked forward to eating something more filling than the rice he had grown accustomed to. John L. recently returned from fighting in the Korean War and he did not come back the same person. John L. was always dutiful, respectful, and obedient which made him the perfect candidate as an American soldier. But after experiencing racism in the military, his virtues were tarnished and his respect for the country and himself was destroyed. This more ruthless side of John L. was revealed subtly through conversation but he kept this side of himself hidden as to not upset the older generation, especially on a day like Christmas.

Next to John L. sat cousin Bobby Hunt, a dark-skinned, chubby teenager. At age 13, he was embracing his rebellious behavior and decided to make a statement by choosing not to dress up like the rest of the family. He stained his shirt as he ate copious amounts of food before anyone even touched their dish. Next to Bobby Hunt sat Wilma's middle sister, Bunny who wore conservative clothing. Unlike John L., Bunny had a lot of faith in America's domestic and foreign policies. She believed that she could make a real difference in the world by helping people, however vague her family thought the notion was.

A large turkey on a silver platter was the focal point for all the seated relatives. A minute had passed since all of the family took their seats. Jack was the closest one to the platter, and a famished Harry wanted to get things moving.

"Jack, can you do the honors?"

Jack snapped out of his daze and the voice of Harry brought him back to reality.

"My pleasure, Pops," replied Jack nonchalantly.

Jack grabbed the large knife by the platter and started carving the turkey. The rest of the family began filling their plates with side dishes. The process reminded Jack of the assembly line he worked on, but much less efficient since he wasn't "in charge."

"Claireece, pour me a glass," commanded Harry.

"Remember what the doctor said?" inquired Claireece, who knew Harry already knew the answer.

"It's a holiday. I can drink a little wine in my own damn house," he declared.

Claireece met Harry halfway and poured Harry half a glass. Jack passed plates of dark meat down to Ricky and Ronnie. No one said a word to each other for a good minute, the sound of the silverware was the only thing breaking the deafening silence.

"Getting all of us television sets was nice, Wilma. Can't say I've used mine though," said Bunny.

"I could come over and show you how it works, Bunny," said Wilma, who saw this as an opportunity to bond with her estranged sister.

"You're probably forgetting the bunny ears," joked Bobby Hunt.

No one laughed but Bobby Hunt. In that moment, Wilma felt disillusioned about how funny her family really was.

"Did Ma tell you, I'm enlisting in the Navy!" said Bunny.

"Wow. Congratulations! When do you..." said Wilma, unable to finish.

"Forget the Navy," interrupted John L.

"Excuse me?" said Bunny angrily.

"Bunch of cowards hiding on a boat."

"Think you're above everyone, Mr. Army Big Shot?" said Bunny.

John L. smirked and took a long a sip of wine. He did not think he was above everyone, just everyone in that room.

"Glad you survived Korea, Johnny Boy" said Harry.

John L. was pleased that his "anti-navy" comment didn't

seem to anger the old folks. His cover wasn't blown.

"Bobby, white or dark?" asked Jack as he continued carving.

"Both," replied Bobby Hunt excitedly.

Jack passed a plate down to Bobby Hunt. He proceeded to stuff his face.

"Bobby, all you do is poop and eat," said Joanne in a snarky tone.

Mild laughter ensued. Wilma now remembered how funny her family could be. Bobby Hunt looked at Joanne briefly, and then continued eating. Wilma cut Ronnie's meat into smaller pieces than what Jack had cut. Jack glared at her as he sliced off a leg.

"Can we change the subject please? Wilma, how is your new shop?" interjected Claireece.

"It's great, Claireece. I love being my own boss."

"John L., white or dark?" asked Jack.

"Dark."

"What are you going to do now that you're back?" asked Joanne.

"Not march for The Man, I'll tell you that. Did enough of that shit in Korea. Maybe I'll move to Detroit," said John L. assertively.

"I'll drink to that," said Jack.

Jack paused his carving to clink his glass with John L.'s. They both took large gulps of wine, subtly implying that they both needed alcohol to get through the family dinner.

"Don't forget the pork, Wilma. Your father slaughtered that pig last week!" stated Claireece.

"Fresh pork, turkey, stuffing, can't beat that with a stick," said Wilma cheerfully.

"Wilma, I know you want white meat," said Jack bluntly.

This affronted Wilma. Jack knew her well enough to know she preferred dark meat over white meat. She knew what he was getting at and she did not appreciate it. Wilma had to come to terms with the fact that Jack was also detached for finding out the truth about her beauty salon. A bitter truth to Jack, which revealed Mr. Silverman, a white man, had helped her financially open up Bailey's and then blindside her with a policy proposal. Jack was ashamed of Wilma's decision and would always find some way to poke her about it. Just like now.

"I want dark, baby," said Wilma firmly.

Jack passed a plate of white meat down to Wilma without anyone else noticing but them. Wilma too was ready for the dinner to be over.

It was New Years Eve and Mr. Silverman's Sherwood Forest Mansion was filled with people dressed in nice suits and dresses. They socialized in a large ballroom, which contained a long buffet table and a bar. "I've Got The World On A String" by Frank Sinatra emanated from what seemed to be the ceiling. Mr. Silverman thought speakers looked tacky and hid them well. Wilma and Jerry were the only black figures in this "snow globe" of a party. Shirley and Jerry talked with a white couple, while Wilma stood next to Shirley, awkwardly.

"Mackinaw is really beautiful," said Shirley to the couple.

"You should come visit our cottage sometime. We plan to retire there," said Jerry.

"We're retiring in Florida," said the white man decisively.

"Winter is just too bitter in Michigan," said the white woman more pleasantly.

Wilma was half-listening for she was too busy savoring the taste of the pickled herring she got from the buffet. She smiled when she saw Mr. Silverman approaching her.

"How is it?" asked Mr. Silverman.

"Delicious. I love herring."

Although it was her first time eating herring, Wilma felt the need to appear more of a food connoisseur in front of the cultured Mr. Silverman.

"I'll get you a bunch of good Jewish recipes from my wife later."

"Where is she? I'd love to meet her."

"She hates these kinds of parties. Jack couldn't make it?"

"You know how he is."

"I think if he met me, he'd like me."

"Not likely. His white boss promoted him and he still doesn't like him."

"That's too bad. I hear you got two new accounts."

"Yeah, those funeral homes are making a pretty penny."

At first, Mr. Silverman was taken aback by the notion of Wilma doing the hair of corpses, but he then thought:

How else could the cadaver's hair look so perfect during those open casket viewings?

A tuxedo-wearing butler held a silver platter with two glasses of champagne. Mr. Silverman took the two glasses and gave one to Wilma. He looked up at the clock and signaled a caterer to turn off the music.

"All right everybody, we're starting the countdown! Get your drinks ready!" yelled Mr. Silverman.

Everyone counted down in unison, loudly.

"Happy New Year!" shouted the crowd at the end of the countdown.

Caterers perched on the upper level of the mansion, released canons of glitter and tinsel that fell like light snow onto the guests. It really did feel like a snow globe now. Wilma gazed upon all of the couples kissing each other. She wondered if Jack would be kissing anyone at his work party. He was always adamant about getting a "New Years kiss" from years past. Mr. Silverman broke Wilma's concentration by clinking his glass with hers. Mr. Silverman chugged his down. Wilma hesitated but then took a sip. From years ago, she remembered alcohol as something that tasted terrible, but this champagne stimulated her taste buds in a good way. Mr. Silverman locked eyes with Wilma and moved in closer toward her. Before Wilma could back away, he kissed her on the cheek. He stepped back and looked into her eyes again.

"Happy New Year, Partner," said Mr. Silverman.

Wilma never thought of Mr. Silverman as her partner, nor, as someone she would allow to invade her personal space.

What did he mean by partner? Does he like me? Do I have feelings for him? thought Wilma.

Those were just a few of the many thoughts that flooded through Wilma's mind that night. The 1960s would be full of changes, not just in Wilma's life, but also on the local, national, and global levels.

For Jack, the New Year started off with a bang. He was

not at a "work party" like he told Wilma. Instead he lay in bed next to Edna, with a white sheet covering their naked bodies.

"Happy New Year, Jack," said Edna gleefully.

Jack returned her elation with a kiss. It was intimacy he had not shown Wilma in months. In Jack's mind, any guilt he had for cheating on her was absolved when she went into business with Mr. Silverman. She trusted a white man over her own husband, and to him, that was unforgivable.

For Joanne, it was a night with friends and a time to babysit the kids. Joanne and six black women socialized in the living area of a small apartment, drinking in between talking. Joanne kneeled down to Ronnie, who was playing with his green army men toys.

"Happy New Year, Ronnie," said Joanne.

She kissed him on the forehead, but he was too preoccupied with his toys to notice. Joanne moved toward Ricky, who wore a party hat to signify himself as the "birthday boy." He was the birthday boy who turned three years old. Ricky sat in front of the television set and watched as Dick Clark appeared on

American Bandstand. Joanne kissed Ricky on the forehead, too.

"Happy New Year, Ricky."

Ricky did not respond either. The large glowing ball on screen mesmerized him. For his birthday, Ricky was a bit melancholy. Before he and Ronnie were dropped off at Joanne's, Wilma and Jack had one of their biggest arguments regarding their New Years Eve plans. It seemed that Wilma and Jack would never be on the same page about "white folk." The parents had set out a cake for Ricky. It was a cake that Ricky ended up eating most of due to the nervous energy that flowed through him during their argument. This would set a trend of Ricky using food as comfort, making him chubbier for his age and the subject of ridicule from Ronnie and other bullies.

For John L., it was just another night of sinning. In a hotel room, he sat on a chair, smoking a cigar while Doreetha performed fellatio on him. Doreetha wore a sparkling red bra and panties. Between puffs, he moaned and climaxed.

"Happy New Year," said Doreetha exasperatedly.

John L. put out his cigar in the ashtray on the dresser. Any pleasure he had was turned off like a switch. His demeanor and tone got more serious as he surveyed the room.

"You know I have to pay for all this shit? You gonna help me?"

"I guess," said Doreetha indecisively.

John L.'s eyes bulged. He couldn't believe what he just heard. He raised his hand and slapped Doreetha across the face, making her ear bleed. This was the first of much abuse; Doreetha was going to receive from John L. To Doreetha, this abuse was not to be considered disgraceful or demoralizing but was part of the job. Her acceptance of that did not negate her pain though.

"What the fuck is this guessing shit?" yelled John L.

He slapped her again, this time with more intensity.

"Yes, I will. You know I will!" shrieked Doreetha.

"Mother fucker, never guess, be sure," demanded John L.

John L. gave her one last slap for good measure. It took every fiber in Doreetha's being not to shed any tears. Tears would warrant more abuse. Between Christmas and New Years, John L. moved to Detroit. During that time he found a hopeless

Doreetha lying on the street. He gave her food, clothing, and a job. She was his first hoe and his reputation of being a "Gorilla Pimp" had been solidified. To Doreetha, John L. was her saving grace. She would be nothing without him. Getting beat up was more appealing than starving on the street. She had to pick her battles so she could win the war that was her dysfunctional life. John L. would always have intimacy issues, but the closest he would ever get to love was spending time with Doreetha. Their relationship was tragic but weren't all love stories? They all end.

Chapter 10: 1960

After eight years of Eisenhower, America seemed to be gravitating to a more youthful presence that popped up in politics. 1960 started off with Massachusetts Senator John F. Kennedy announcing his candidacy for the democratic nomination for President. In a few short months he would win his party's nomination, and begin a ruthless campaign against Vice President Richard Nixon that would lead to one of the closest elections in American history.

At Bailey's Salon, Wilma, Janette, and Bryce styled the hair of their black women clients while Anita swept the floor. It was a normal spring afternoon for Bailey's: bustling with clients and patrons running the numbers. It was never a dull moment.

"Hear those gunshots over on Dexter?" asked Janette's client.

"No," replied Janette.

"Two colored boys were killed by the police," said the client as she shook her head during Janette's pause from styling.

Bryce famously eavesdropped and felt inclined to put his

two cents in the conversation jar.

"I'm sick of these racist cops," said Bryce dramatically.

"Amen to that!" said Anita.

"We need more colored cops is what we need," said the client.

"What about that new Kennedy guy?" asked Anita.

"Yeah, he's supposed to be good for us 'colored folks,' we'll have to wait and see." interjected Wilma sarcastically.

Kathy entered the shop.

"How was Diggs?" asked Wilma.

"Once I got used to the fact that they don't talk back, it was okay. The families were pleased," said Kathy.

"Thank you for doing this, Kathy."

"It's just another head of hair," said Kathy.

Kathy had grown up a lot in the last year. She perfected her own style and got along great with the clients. Wilma had no doubt that she could do a good job on the cadavers. Initially, Wilma was going to spearhead the Diggs and Swanson Funeral Home accounts personally, but with all of the traffic coming in with the numbers, she decided to stay close to the shop.

The entrance bell rang and Mr. Silverman walked in, wearing his gray suit. Bryce took note of his balding head and decided it was his chance to joke with the "Old Man" as he referred to him as.

"We got that wig all curled and set for you, Mr. Silverman," said Bryce jokingly.

"Bryce, when I need a wig, I'll let you know," retorted Mr. Silverman.

Wilma said goodbye to her newly styled client and hello to her "partner."

"Got a minute?" asked Mr. Silverman.

Wilma nodded and led him to the backroom. They walked in on Kim curling a wig.

"Take a break, Kim," said Wilma.

Kim scurried out of the room, keeping as much distance as she could from Mr. Silverman. Kim feared people she didn't know and had no interest in getting to know them.

"Come with me to the track tonight. You can bet some of that money you're making on the ponies."

"I promised Jack a family dinner tonight. How about tomorrow?"

"We'll see...I noticed your car isn't parked outside today. Something wrong?"

"No, Jack needed the car today."

"Let me drive you home at least."

It was only a twenty-minute walk home, but after being on her feet all day, it always seemed longer. She agreed to the offer but thought about how Jack would react if he saw her come home with Mr. Silverman. To him, it was bad enough that she worked with him but accepting rides might be another issue. Wilma was a grown woman though and was not about to let Jack's skewed perception of white people dictate her life. Piercing through her thoughts was Mr. Silverman's subsequent comment.

"There's other things we need to talk about," he said ominously.

Ricky and Ronnie wrestled in the living room while Jack watched news footage of John F. Kennedy and Richard Nixon campaigning throughout the country on the television set. An uninterested Jack slouched on the couch and drank from a bottle of gin. His stress stemmed from his long workdays and the two women in his life working long hours into the night.

"Where the hell is your mother?" mumbled Jack.

Ricky and Ronnie ignored their father and continued wrestling. A chubby Ricky sat on Ronnie, subduing him.

"I win!" declared Ricky proudly.

"Get your fat butt off of me," said Ronnie.

Jack didn't have to look back to assess the situation. If there was ever any conflict between Ricky and Ronnie, Ronnie was always at fault.

"Ronnie, leave Ricky alone before I whoop your ass."

Jack heard something. It was a noise he was far too familiar with. Jack got up and walked to the front window. He looked outside and gazed upon the origin of the noise; the engine of a green Chrysler Imperial that pulled into the driveway. His eyes were drawn to the blonde streak in Wilma's hair. Wilma was seated in the passenger seat and Mr. Silverman was at the wheel.

Jack clenched his fist and started breathing heavily.

"Go to your room. Now!" yelled Jack.

Ricky and Ronnie ran out of the living room, fearfully.

In the car, Mr. Silverman smoked a cigarette, flicking the ashes out the window.

"Cops?" inquired Wilma.

"Not exactly Detroit's finest," responded Mr. Silverman.

"You trust them?"

"We have an understanding."

Wilma hoped that this "understanding" would not falter and end up putting Wilma into a jail cell. But she would never reveal such fears to her business partner. Mr. Silverman flicked the cigarette out the window.

"Old folk playing the numbers is one thing, but cops and politicians?"

"You'll just be getting a little more volume at the shop. Nothing you can't handle."

Mr. Silverman looked out through the windshield and saw Jack staring at them from the front window, a curtain only partially blocking him. Mr. Silverman smiled.

"Thanks for the ride, Silverman."

"Anytime, Wilma."

Wilma exited the car and walked up to the house. Mr. Silverman made eye contact with Jack and waved at him before pulling off. Jack covered the window with the curtain and threw his gin bottle against the wall, shattering it loudly. Jack ran to the dresser drawer next to the front door and pulled out his silver gun. Wilma opened the door and Jack slammed her face with the butt of the weapon. She fell to the ground in front of the door, nose gushing blood. Ronnie and Ricky ran in and stared at their fallen mother.

"Mama!" shrieked Ronnie.

"Stay back, baby," said Wilma protectively.

Ricky watched her in shock while Ronnie cried. They stood behind the couch, keeping their distance from a hyperventilating Jack.

"You fucking him?" yelled Jack.

Wilma slowly tried to stand up. Her concern became less

about her and more about her children. She needed to calm him down. He had to believe her.

"Please, baby. No! Please!" she screamed.

"Don't lie to me!"

Jack hit the back of the Wilma's head with the gun. Ronnie shrieked again as Wilma fell back to the ground, now unconscious. Blood dripped from the gun that was shaking in Jack's hand. Ronnie remained hidden behind the couch but Ricky walked over cautiously and crouched by his bleeding mother.

"Mama!" yelled Ricky at a nonresponsive Wilma.

Jack stared into Ricky's scared and innocent eyes. Jack was still trembling. He trudged over to the front dresser and opened the drawer. Without saying a word, he wiped off the blood with a rag and placed the gun back in the drawer. Ronnie joined Ricky by Wilma's unconscious body. Jack ignored them and walked to the kitchen. He calmly washed the blood off of his hands, tuning out the faint crying from Ronnie. Jack dried his hands and picked up the telephone. He dialed a number.

About ten minutes later, the recipient of the phone call:

Joanne, parked across the street from Wilma and Jack's house. Parked in the driveway was an ambulance. Joanne ran to the house and witnessed Wilma's body being loaded into the ambulance. Joanne only got a brief glimpse, but the bandages on Wilma's nose and head confirmed that she indeed had a "bad accident" as Jack described to her.

At the doorway stood two middle-aged cops, one black and one white. They faced Jack, whose back leaned against the gun drawer. Joanne walked up and made eye contact with Jack.

"They're on the couch," said Jack flatly.

Joanne didn't say anything as she walked into the house. She hugged Ricky and Ronnie tightly.

"Who's that?" asked the White Cop.

"Her sister," said Jack.

"Why is she here?"

"Pick up my kids."

"Jack, right?" asked the Black Cop.

Jack nodded. He was partially concerned that Joanne could hear the conversation but he knew it really didn't matter.

"Walk us through what happened" stated the Black cop.

"We had a fight. A misunderstanding...I pushed her a little too hard and she hit her head."

The White Cop raised his eyebrows, skeptical of the tale. Joanne led Ricky and Ronnie out of the house. The kids kept their heads down as Joanne glared at Jack, indicating that she indeed heard what he said.

"Bye, kids!" called out Jack.

Ricky and Ronnie didn't turn their heads back as Joanne walked them to her car.

"I think we've got enough information for the report," said the Black Cop. The White Cop nodded in agreement, putting his skepticism aside so he could go home. They exited the house. Jack contemplated cleaning the messy living room but that thought was trumped by the thought of calling Edna.

I need to unwind, he thought.

A week later, Wilma had still not returned home. She sought refuge at Joanne's with her sons and had no contact with Jack. She sat in between Ronnie and Ricky on the couch and watched *The Ed Sullivan Show* as Joanne washed dishes in the kitchen. The front door was kicked in suddenly. Jack sprinted to the couch and before anyone could react, he picked up an expressionless Ricky and ran out of the house with him. Ronnie started wailing. Joanne entered after hearing the noise.

"Oh my god. What happened?" yelled Joanne.

All Wilma could do in that moment was stare in shock at the kicked in door. Her son was gone. He was kidnapped by a man she no longer wanted anything to do with.

I have to get Ricky back, she thought.

An hour later, Jack sat on a chair on one end of the living room while Ricky sat on the couch on the other end. They peered into each other's eyes blankly. Jack didn't know what to say. He wasn't about to apologize because in his mind Wilma deserved it. Ricky's attention diverted to a bowl of peanuts on the table that separated them. He grabbed the bowl and ran into his room.

A cab pulled up outside the house. Before exiting, Wilma turned to the driver and extended her hand to him.

"There's another ten. Wait for me," she said.

She handed the driver the money, exited the cab, and approached her house that had now lost all glamour.

Wilma opened the unlocked front door and found Jack sitting with his legs crossed.

"Where is he?" asked Wilma nervously.

"He's in his room," replied Jack.

Wilma cautiously walked toward Ricky's room. Jack stood up and got in her way.

"Why didn't you come home after the hospital?"

Wilma trembled and inched back as he moved in closer. She realized in that moment that she could no longer be intimate with this man again. Ricky would be their only child. She decided to humor him to avoid another beating.

"We all need time, Jack."

"You know I love you and Ricky."

"What about Ronnie?" asked Wilma assertively.

"I told Joanne to take the boys for just that night. Here we are a week later, all of you hiding out."

Jack walked to the kitchen table and placed down two

documents with a pen on top.

"Sign these," commanded Jack.

Wilma walked to the table and studied the papers, as Jack hovered over her.

"You want everything," said Wilma surprisingly.

"Just the mortgage and the insurance policies. I already took the rest of the money out the joint account."

Wilma gave a smirk that said: *of course you did.*

"If I sign these, you're gonna let me take my son, right?"

"Yeah, but I'm keeping the car."

Wilma could not believe that Jack compared his son to a car. The man she fell in love with was gone. She hesitated and then, without looking over the documents, she signed them. She threw down the pen and walked briskly to Ricky's bedroom door.

"Ricky! Baby, it's Mama. Open up."

Ricky opened the door slowly and he threw himself into his mother's arms.

"Come on, baby. Let's go."

Wilma held Ricky close as they neared the front door.

"Ricky," said Jack commandingly.

Ricky latched himself to Wilma's leg, not looking at Jack.

"Say bye to your daddy." said Wilma firmly.

Ricky refused to acknowledge Jack. Jack wasn't proud of this but he understood that his son was closer to his mother than his father. This was a consequence of his violent actions. He wasn't about to force love from his child. If anything, he knew he would come back to him once Wilma's "deal with The Devil" came to a head. He was counting on it.

Wilma and Ricky walked out of the house.

"God damn it," said Wilma.

The cab was gone and it meant a twenty-block walk for her and Ricky. They began their trek on the sidewalk. Tears streamed down her cheeks but she wiped them off quickly. She did not want to be weak in front of a boy she wanted to grow up to be strong. Wilma kept her composure for those twenty blocks and they arrived at Joanne's an hour later.

Ricky and Ronnie stuffed their faces at Joanne's kitchen table while Wilma and Joanne discussed their next moves. Wilma was hungry too but knew she wouldn't be able to eat.

"You have to call the police," said Joanne.

"Forget the cops. They didn't do nothing to Jack."

"Kidnapping is different, Wilma. They might not have sympathy for a woman but they would for a child."

"How can you kidnap your own kid?" said Wilma.

Joanne had no response to this. Although Jack's methodology was malicious, Ricky was still his son and any legal action would probably not stick.

"It's done. In the morning I'm getting a lawyer and filing for divorce," said Wilma, although she could not believe what she had just said.

It was bad enough leaving Barney but leaving Jack would be different. It was the closest thing to a normal family unit Wilma ever had. As Wilma uttered the word "divorce" she feared that she would never marry again and that happiness in an emotional relationship seemed like a distant dream. Wilma's pessimism was faded when she looked out the window and saw a cab pull up. She walked into the kitchen to round up her kids.

Joanne disagreed with Wilma's next move.

"You just walked twenty blocks to get here. At least stay the night," said Joanne.

"It's too risky."

The thought of Wilma and her sons being asleep when Jack felt the need to "see" his son again, haunted Wilma. She kept reliving the earlier calamity in her head. Jack broke down the door. Jack took Ricky. Wilma felt hopeless. If Wilma hated anything in life it was feeling hopeless. Now was the time to take control. Wilma fetched the coats from the closet and put one on Ricky while Ronnie put on his own.

"Where will you go?" asked Joanne.

"Somewhere Jack doesn't know about," replied Wilma.

"Where Wilma? What if I need to get in touch with you?"

"We'll be at Shirley's."

Jack never liked Shirley because of the lifestyle she had and how it became part of Wilma's. He always kept a comfortable distance from anything that had to do with Shirley. Wilma was pretty sure he did not know her last name, which made Shirley's seem like a safe haven for her sons, just as it was after Barney went off the edge. Wilma hoped this would be the last time she would have to ask Shirley for help. She had already done so much. Desperate times call for desperate measures and for the first time in a long time, Wilma Bailey felt desperate.

It was a beautiful spring day at Hazel Park Raceway. Nine men on horses raced around a circular track. The loud stampeding hooves and the cheering crowd permeated throughout the stadium. Black and white people alike yelled out different numbers and names associated with their bets. Mr. Silverman, Moe, and Jeremy; a skinny red headed, white man, entered the stadium, dressed to impress. Behind them were Wilma and Shirley. Wilma stared in awe at a spectacle that she had never seen before. Shirley wasn't impressed for she had spent many days at Hazel. The group climbed the stairs to a box seat that gave them the perfect aerial view of the track. As they sat down, Shirley studied Moe and Jeremy standing behind Mr. Silverman.

"They don't talk much do they?" asked Shirley.

"They're not paid to talk," replied Mr. Silverman.

Moe and Jeremy did not flinch or acknowledge the conversation. They kept their eyes on the raceway in front of them. Wilma peered out at the horses and jockeys prepping to race. Between all of the numbers she recorded daily at the salon, Wilma finally got to see the method behind the madness. It was lucrative. People loved these races, especially Mr. Silverman.

"Who'd you bet on?" asked Wilma.

"The winners," said Mr. Silverman bluntly.

"You're psychic now, huh?" joked Wilma.

"I just have good instincts."

"Which ones are gonna win then?"

"It's gonna be 4, 8, 5 combination."

Wilma examined each of the horses on the track, taking note of their respective number and jockey.

"I learned long ago never to bet against *Maximilian* over here," declared Shirley.

Mr. Silverman darted his gaze at Shirley. It was like the temperature in the box seat heated up in that moment. Before words were uttered, Wilma sensed the tension between the two.

"Shirley, didn't I ask you not to call me that?" said Mr. Silverman sternly.

Shirley stood in the booth, awkwardly. She had remembered that Mr. Silverman never wanted to be called by his first name. She never knew why but it was a trigger for him. Shirley decided to remove herself from the conflict before saying something else to escalate it.

"I'm gonna get a hot dog. Either of you want anything?"

Wilma shook her head no and Mr. Silverman ignored her. Shirley left the box, remembering the lesson that "Maximilian" was off limits. Mr. Silverman studied Wilma's face.

"You're healing up nicely," said Mr. Silverman.

Wilma hated talking about what happened and was mad at Shirley for opening her big mouth to Mr. Silverman. He was her business partner and the last thing she wanted to do was to project weakness or have him concern himself with Jack.

"Have you heard from him?" he asked.

"No," replied Wilma.

"Say the word, Wilma and he'll never be a problem

again."

Never be a problem again? thought Wilma.

Mr. Silverman had always been a mysterious man. He owned a commercial laundry and the only illegal business she knew he dabbled in was all of the gambling at the shop, but he just suggested murder. Wilma could not brush off this comment and needed to keep him grounded.

"What? That's Ricky's father."

"Come on Wilma, you think I'd fuckin' hurt somebody?"

The loud sound of the gates opening pierced the arena, causing Wilma to jump.

"And they're off!" yelled The Announcer over the loudspeaker.

Wilma did not want to answer his question truthfully because she was unsure of what this man was capable of. He was generous, charming, and nice but Wilma had good instincts too and they told her that he could be more dangerous than she originally thought. Mr. Silverman gauged how uncomfortable Wilma was. He smiled and looked onto the raceway.

Shirley had retreated to the hot dog stand. She thought that Mr. Silverman's stare would catch her on fire if she stayed in that box seat any longer. She figured it would be best to let him cool off a little before showing her face again. Shirley squirted mustard on her hot dog with ease but struggled with the ketchup. She shook the bottle several times until a huge glob of ketchup shot out of the bottle, some of it staining her dress.

"Damn it!" she exclaimed.

Shirley scrubbed her dress with a wet towel, determined to remove the stain. A tall white man with a mustache stared at Shirley from the other side of the stand. He wore a black suit and a black hat with a red rose on his lapel. As Shirley cleaned off her hot dog and began to walk away, she made eye contact with the mustached man. Unbeknownst to her husband Jerry, she was always one to flirt whenever she had the chance, especially with strangers. She seductively put the hot dog in her mouth and then took a giant bite. The mustached man smirked at this. Shirley winked and walked away.

Shirley entered the box seat, consuming the last bite of

her hot dog. Wilma was seated alone, Mr. Silverman and his "henchmen" nowhere to be found.

"Where did he go?" asked Shirley.

"He said he had business to attend to," replied Wilma.

"Only he would still do business after winning at the races."

"How'd you know he won?"

Shirley gave a look to Wilma that was interpreted as a sarcastic "come on." Wilma realized that Mr. Silverman's "good instincts" were not the most natural. Wilma learned later that Mr. Silverman had his hands in everything.

Moe and Jeremy stood on both sides of the bathroom entrance, awaiting their boss to finish his "business." Mr. Silverman concluded said "business" at the urinal and adjusted his tie in the mirror. Suddenly, the mustached man swung open one of the stall doors and swiftly pressed a 45 automatic firearm to Mr. Silverman's head. The hateful assailant pulled the trigger but the gun jammed. Mr. Silverman was a Jewish man who believed in a higher power and that belief became even more solidified after cheating fate in that moment.

"Guys!" yelled Mr. Silverman loudly.

The mustached man cocked the gun again, intending to blow Mr. Silverman's brains all over the bathroom mirror. His intention changed when Jeremy ran in, holding his pistol. The assailant fired the round into Jeremy's chest. Blood splattered everywhere. Moe arrived a split second later and shot the mustached man in the leg. His scream was drowned out by the stampede of horses. The mustached man fell to the floor, trying to hold back his agony. Moe ran over and pointed his gun at the assailant's head. As the subdued aggressor breathed heavily and moaned in pain, Mr. Silverman calmly washed Jeremy's blood off of his face. He stepped over Jeremy's corpse and faced Moe, who had his gun now pressed to the man's head. Mr. Silverman glared at his failed assassin.

"Keep him alive," said Mr. Silverman curtly.

"Fuck you, Jew!" yelled the mustached man.

Mr. Silverman had been discriminated for being Jewish his whole life. When he was younger, he thought his background was a weakness. He almost believed that being "a Jew" was a lesser being. He drew strength from his father, who embraced being Jewish in a confident and powerful way. Mr. Silverman's father was a member of the Purple Gang; a prominent Jewish mob of bootleggers and hijackers that controlled Detroit's vice, gambling, liquor, and drug trade during prohibition in the 1920s. Mr. Silverman learned how to be tough from his father. He even shadowed him on some of his father's illegal jobs. Mr. Silverman transformed the stigma of "Jew" from a weakness to a strength because of his father. He also learned how to remain calm after there was an attempt on one's life. A skill he had mastered from his life experiences.

"You should really be more polite to the people who hold your life in their hands." said Mr. Silverman collectedly.

Mr. Silverman gave a slight head nod that Moe understood completely. Moe slammed his pistol across the man's face, breaking his nose. Mr. Silverman bent down to Jeremy's corpse and fished out his wallet and grabbed his gun.

"I know who sent you. Tell him to sign the Union contract

or you're gonna be paying a very high insurance premium. Either way you're gonna pay us," said Mr. Silverman to the bleeding assaulter.

The man moaned in pain, blood from his nose soaked into his mustache. Moe pistol-whipped him unconscious. Mr. Silverman took the red rose off of the attacker's lapel and put it on his own. Dave, the Security Director at Hazel Park, walked into the bathroom.

"Not again," said Dave grumpily.

"The one closest to you is still alive. Drop him at the usual spot," instructed Mr. Silverman.

Mr. Silverman handed Dave a wad of cash. Dave did not need to count it or think twice before stuffing the money into his front pocket and pulling out black trash bags from his back one. Mr. Silverman and Moe returned to the box seat to rejoin Wilma and Shirley.

"Ladies, I'm afraid I won't be able to join you for the next race. But you are welcome to stay here and enjoy all of the amenities."

"You're important. We get it," said Shirley smugly.

Shirley then noticed streaks of blood on Mr. Silverman's sleeve. She nervously made eye contact with him as Wilma moved in closer. Shirley connected the dots on the type of business he had indeed attended to.

"Hey this was fun. Thanks," said Wilma.

Wilma moved in and hugged Mr. Silverman. She too bore witness to the red stains on Mr. Silverman's dress shirt.

"Is that...blood?" asked Wilma nervously.

Shirley stood up quickly and thought even quicker for the sake of maintaining their collective business relationship. After all, it was a relationship that was yielding large profits.

"Isn't that ketchup bottle a doozy? I almost ruined my blouse trying to do my hot dog," said an intervening Shirley.

Mr. Silverman smiled and nodded which he thought would legitimize Shirley's claim, but Wilma didn't buy it. If it was ketchup, it meant Mr. Silverman was clumsy. If it was blood, then perhaps he was capable of violence that could very well infect their business relationship.

Chapter 11: 1963 (Part Two)

A lot had changed in the three years leading up to John L.'s arrival at Bailey's that evening of June 11, 1963. The leader of the free world now appeared to be more of an advocate for Civil Rights. Before he was even elected, John F. Kennedy and his brother Robert Kennedy made arrangements to release Martin Luther King Jr. from jail. Although some argue this was a politically fueled move to secure the black vote, Kennedy was deemed to be more sympathetic toward the concept of "equality for all." When he was in office, he sent in federal marshals to protect the Freedom Riders from mob violence. Kennedy had also appointed the first Negro to the U.S. District Court; a Detroit native named Wade McCree.

Kennedy's address, that Ricky turned off that night, proposed legislation that would change the Negro life forever with regards to equal access to schools and greater protection at the polls, which would give blacks a sense of entitlement that would eventually be a double-edged sword for the city of Detroit. Wilma's business boomed in those three years. She not only had a loyal clientele, but Bailey's became the best place to make your bets for anyone on the socioeconomic spectrum. From the homeless in rags to the executives in suits, Wilma was getting exposure like never before. Mr. Silverman had friends in law enforcement, which made Wilma untouchable. Wilma soon got over her guilty conscience regarding the illegality of "number running." Her receptionist had enough though and put her notice in. Wilma was left with no one she could trust to do the numbers. That day, John L. insisted that he could help.

Ronnie was on his knees, soaking up the dark Pepsi beverage with the white towels delivered by Moe only a few hours earlier. Ronnie did not like the way Moe looked at him but also did not trust the man. Ronnie oddly felt a level of satisfaction, staining Moe's white towels with the dark liquid. Dexter sipped some of the drink but John L. was quick to yank him away by his collar.

"Wilma, I hear you're taking the numbers," said John L.

"As long as you got cash, your credit's no good here," joked Wilma.

"My girl Doreetha is looking for a job. She could help you out."

"One of your girls?" asked Wilma skeptically.

Ricky was bored with the conversation between Wilma and John L. He was more entertained by watching Ronnie clean up the spill. Ricky then decided to take the high road and help his brother wipe up the mess. Maybe that would limit the hazing.

"Doreetha will be as loyal to you as Dexter is to me," said John L.

Wilma looked down at Dexter who was seated calmly next to John L.'s leg. Wilma was overwhelmed. She would feel guilty if she made one of her stylists record the numbers. That would be wasting their time when they should be honing their cosmetic skills. With Doreetha joining the workforce, Wilma would not have to stop in the middle of doing hair to take the damn numbers. Before Wilma could even express her interest, John L. made a decision.

"I'll bring her in. Just talk to her."

That's the kind of guy John L. was. He was a man of

action who always steered any conversation to his liking. John L. locked eyes with Kathy across the salon as she swept up hair on the floor. He waltzed over to her and Dexter devotedly followed. John L. appreciated beauty when he saw it. Kathy was the prettiest girl in the shop, besides Wilma of course.

"How you doin', sugar?" asked John L. flirtatiously.

"I'm good. Who are you?" replied Kathy.

Wilma knew what John L. was doing and she would not allow it. The last thing she would need was John L. renting space in one of her beautician's heads. Wilma had faith in the moral compass of her workers, but she knew Kathy was the most impressionable. She walked over to them briskly.

"Kathy, meet my cousin, John L. John L. meet Kathy. She's *engaged*," said Wilma firmly.

Kathy excitedly lifted up her hand to show a small diamond ring on her finger.

"I'm sorry, darling. Take it as a compliment," said John L. smoothly.

If John L. was sure about anything, it was that he would

never get married or expose himself to the vulnerability and the weakness that was "love." Janette led a "Diana Ross looking" Ruby to the counter to check her out. Janette bent down to pet Dexter on her journey. She made eye contact with John L. before his eyes moved down slowly like an old elevator, taking in every level of Janette's body. Janette knew what he was doing and ignored him. She checked out Ruby and John L. moved in closer to Janette as she completed the transaction.

"Damn, Janette, you're fine," said John L.

"No."

"Can I take you out tonight?"

"Get away from me, John L. Wilma!"

Janette returned to her station and Wilma gave John L. a menacing glare. John L. smiled and nodded, getting the message.

"I'll go out with you tonight," chimed in Bryce.

Bryce did his one leg lean and winked at John L. Bryce was out and proud and could not keep his eyes of John L. the entire time he was in the shop. If there was one group of people John L. hated more than the Asians, it was the gays. He had no problem with the closeted and reserved types, but the flamboyant and loud ones like Bryce, bothered the shit out of him. Besides, there was not a big enough market for male prostitutes, thus Bryce was just a useless annoyance to him.

"F off," yelled John L.

"F you too, oh my god," said Bryce dramatically.

"Watch the language in my shop!" declared Wilma.

The yelling prompted Dexter to growl and yelp loudly.

"All right, baby. I'm gone," said John L.

"Okay, see you later!" yelled Bryce from the back.

"I'm not talking to you. Bye, Wilma," said John L. curtly.

John L. walked out with Dexter following beside him. As he exited, a nappy-headed Negro woman entered the salon and approached the counter. Wilma realized that she was a new customer and got excited. She studied her hair and thought of all the endless possibilities that could turn her beautiful.

"Welcome to Bailey's," said Wilma proudly.

"Put me down for a dollar on 1-9-4," said the woman.

The Nappy Woman set a dollar on the counter, swiftly.

Wilma sighed before taking it. If Wilma had someone taking the numbers, her focus would be more on her stylistic passion. She would only deal with the people she wanted to: the clients. John L.'s girl Doreetha would make things easier at the shop.

But can I trust a prostitute? I can trust John L. He's a Miller. And Millers and Baileys look out for each other.

John L. drove slowly down Woodward Avenue in his white Cadillac, as Dexter tried to stay stationary on the leather back seat. John L. rolled down the window and gazed upon 20 to 30 prostitutes on the sidewalk, wearing fishnets and high heels. He stopped the car next to the sidewalk where Doreetha stood promiscuously.

"Get in," commanded John L.

Like Dexter, Doreetha obediently complied. She opened the door and sat in the front seat. She did not get as many clients as she wanted so avoiding a confrontation with John L. was a priority for her. But a beating was probably inevitable.

"I want you dressed your best. We're going to The 20 Grand tonight," said John L.

Located at the intersection of 14th Street and Warren Avenue, The 20 Grand was one of Detroit's most famous nightclubs. It was a facility that had it all; live performances, a bowling alley, a studio, and a motel. It was a place of escapism for the Negro. That summer night, The Supremes performed "My Heart Can't Take It No More." Diana Ross' hair was styled just how Wilma had described it to Janette. The large club was filled with Negroes in suits and dresses. Producer Berry Gordy Jr. admired his artists from the front row. In a few short years, Gordy would establish Motown Records as one of the most successful independent record companies in the country. He had a talent of attracting the best songwriters, musicians, and producers. In 1963, The Supremes were gaining momentum. Their songs especially touched audiences on a local level. Doreetha, in a purple dress, bobbed her head, relating to the pain present in the song.

"Stop hurting me

Now don't you think you're overdoing it?

I still care I must admit," sang Diana Ross beautifully.

Doreetha glanced at John L., hoping the lyrics would cause him to reflect on his own behavior, but he sat next to her indifferent. All John L. could think about was money as he stared at Berry Gordy. He related to him in that moment. Gordy was making money off of his girls too. The only difference was the service the women offered. Berry Gordy marketed his girl's voices. John L. marketed his girl's bodies. To John L., prostituting women were means to an end, a financial end.

Outside the club, in an alley, a built black man had a similar mindset to John L. but favored a more violent approach in his business model. His name was Big Nick, a gangster pimp that was known for his wide variety of prostitutes. His customers joked that Big Nick had a girl for every pound of weight he had. In the alley, Big Nick was not selling his product. Instead he was punishing someone for losing "a pound" that day. He clenched the throat of a skinnier black man, pushing him against the wall of The 20 Grand. When the man's face started turning the same color as Doreetha's dress, Big Nick let go and pushed him into a pile of garbage bags.

"How do you like to be choked out?" asked Big Nick angrily.

"It was an accident. I didn't think she would..." replied the skinny man exasperatedly.

Big Nick did not care if it "was an accident" or what he "thought would happen." He wanted compensation and retribution for the prostitute this pervert killed.

"Please, Nick. I'll get you the money Monday when the banks open."

Big Nick remained silent and stoic. The skinny man got on his knees in the pile of rubbish and hoped Big Nick would understand the predicament he was in.

"I gotta pay my bookie back first. They threatened my kids, man."

"Oh, yeah? Mother fucker!"

Big Nick pulled out a revolver from his jacket.

"No! Please!"

Big Nick slammed the gun into the man's face as the tumbler exploded out onto the concrete. The skinny man fell back onto the trash heap, blood gushing from his forehead. Big Nick reached into the pocket, of the now unconscious man, and pulled out a wad of cash. It was the cash he stole from the murdered prostitute along with his own earnings. Big Nick walked in through the side door of the club, leaving the man to bleed out.

The Supremes were just leaving the stage as Big Nick walked in. John L. saw Big Nick from across the club. As the two pimps made eye contact, John L. waved two fingers to signal him to come over. Big Nick approached the table, paying more attention to John L.'s "arm ornament."

"What am I, your fuckin' dog?" said Big Nick as he sat at the table with them.

"I could never feed your ass," retorted John L.

Big Nick stared at Doreetha with an expression of desire. Doreetha kept her head down, avoiding eye contact with Big Nick because if a hoe ever made eye contact with another pimp, beatings were in order.

"This must be the finest girl I've seen you with," said Big Nick charmingly.

Doreetha was in between a rock; John L. and a hard place; Big Nick. She felt that anything she did whether it was subtly or explicitly would be the wrong thing so she decided to pry herself from between them.

"I'm gonna freshen up. Be right back, baby," said Doreetha to John L.

Doreetha kissed John L. on the cheek and walked toward the back of the club. Big Nick made a point to turn around and watch her leave. Big Nick was always an "ass man" over a "boobs man" and any girl he recruited, reflected that preference. He turned back to face John L. and stir the waters a little bit.

"She looked me dead in the eye. You be careful, John L."

"She didn't look you in no fuckin' eye. Get your own bitches."

"You know I have them in spades, Big Pimpin."

John L. smirked knowing Big Nick had double the girls that John L. had. John L. tended to feel like he was at a lower level than Big Nick. There was always an unspoken competition between them, but they never let it get in the way of their friendship. It was this friendship that allowed John L. to even think about suggesting what he was about propose. He leaned in closer to Big Nick.

"I know how to get us some money," said John L. softly.

Big Nick stared at John L. skeptically. With the mob breathing down their neck and women being too afraid to walk the streets at night, pimping was not as lucrative as it used to be. Big Nick could see in John L.'s eyes that he was excited about something, something that could be beneficial to both of them. Big Nick purposefully did not respond, because he wanted John L. to show all of his cards before he would even show one of his.

"It's all about the numbers, baby," said John L.

Big Nick only nodded and smirked, still not saying a word. John L. realized that Big Nick was not going to ask any follow-up questions so he decided to shoot one off first.

"Ever hear of Bailey's Salon?"

"Your cousin's shop," said Big Nick flatly.

Before John L. could delve into his plan, Doreetha returned to the table. John L. smiled at Big Nick before acknowledging Doreetha.

"Are you ready to make some real money, baby?" asked John L.

Doreetha made sure not to look at Big Nick as she nodded hesitantly to John L. Doreetha had never been in a situation where one pimp discussed making money in front of another pimp. She knew that John L. and Big Nick were friends, but John L.'s comment was crossing a line that she thought would never be crossed in this business.

"Ever hear of Bailey's Salon, baby?" asked John L.

Doreetha had heard of Bailey's Salon. It was the most popular place to get one's hair done in Detroit. Doreetha never stepped foot in Bailey's since she had a friend who would do her hair for free. She often considered taking her appearance to a different level by going to Bailey's, but decided to stay loyal to her friend. In that moment, Doreetha chose not to reveal her familiarity with Bailey's Salon, hoping that John L. would present his brainchild more quickly. The three of them talked at that table until dawn, putting a plan in motion that would change the course of their lives forever.

The next day at Bailey's, Anita, Kathy, and Janette all styled the hair of their respective clients. It was a quieter day; everyone kept to themselves. The entrance bell rang and sliced the silence. It was John L., who appeared stylish as always. He wore a baby blue suit with shoes of the same color. Holding his arm like a prom date was Doreetha. She wore a bright red shirt and shorts, which was not an outfit skimpy enough to convey promiscuity, yet not conservative enough to convey professionalism. The colorful lovers approached the counter. Just as they stopped there, John L. leaned in and whispered to Doreetha.

"Just smile and nod," he said.

Doreetha nodded. Wilma walked out of the backroom between Bryce and Kim yelling at each other. This was definitely not the first time the two of them caused unnecessary drama.

"You best not steal my shears again!" yelled Bryce.

"My shears," said Kim curtly.

"Kim, they are Bryce's shears. Kathy and Janette saw you

take them from his station," said Wilma.

Kim eyed Kathy and Janette for "snitching." The stylists refused to make eye contact with Kim. Kim could have been honest and just given the shears back, but she had asked Wilma for new shears for weeks and Wilma always forgot. Stealing Bryce's was an example of "survival of the fittest" in her mind. She lied through her yellow teeth.

"No I no steal. Someone else."

"Who else? A kamikaze pilot just swooped in and took 'em?

Bryce's ignorance was showing. Kamikazes were suicide attacks by Japanese against the Allies in World War II. Bryce did not know or care. Much like John L., to Bryce, all Asians were the same. Kim did not react kindly to this comment. She proceeded to angrily yell at Bryce in Korean. As she moved in toward Bryce, Wilma stood in her way to prevent anything from becoming physical.

"Ching chong ling long to you too!" yelled Bryce.

Kim, understanding that Wilma would not allow her to

take a shot at Bryce, ran into the backroom. She ran back out with her handbag. She proceeded to smoke a cigarette outside the shop. Bryce returned to his workstation, smugly. Wilma exhaled deeply and felt like she had just dealt with one of Ronnie and Ricky's conflicts. She approached the counter and studied Doreetha. Wilma was not impressed with the outfit she chose for a job interview. She broke the ice by calling attention to what had just happened with her staff.

"It's hard finding good help these days. So, you must be Doreetha," said Wilma.

Wilma extended her hand for a handshake. Doreetha hesitantly shook her hand, a gesture she rarely used in her life. Wilma could sense her nervousness and decided to refrain from being too judgmental or harsh on the girl.

"Let's go in the back where it's more private," said Wilma.

Wilma led them into the backroom and moved all of the wigs and supplies off of a circular table. John L.'s face contorted, as he smelled Kim's Korean rice dish that sat on the counter.

With smell being the strongest sense tied to memory, John L. immediately thought of his traumas from the war. He kept his pain internal, as he always did.

"John L. says you are willing to work here and help out with some things around the shop," said Wilma.

Doreetha followed her pimp's instructions and just smiled and nodded. Wilma expected more of a response so she went the questioning route.

"Why do you want this job?" asked Wilma.

Doreetha looked at John L. and hoped that he would give her the answer so she did not have to break his rule. John L. raised his eyebrows, which indicated that she needed to say something. Doreetha bowed her head for a second and then tilted it back up.

"I just need a change," said Doreetha sincerely.

Wilma saw the tiredness in Doreetha's eyes. Wilma did not know any details of Doreetha's relationship with her cousin, but she knew this job would be better than a life on the street. Wilma wanted her to realize the importance of getting this job.

"This job requires you to do a lot of counting and inventory. Do you think you can handle that?" asked Wilma.

"Math was my best subject in school," replied Doreetha.

"You graduate?"

"Got up to be a sophomore."

"John L. says I can trust you."

"He'll kill me if I mess up," said Doreetha lightheartedly.

Doreetha hided her honesty behind her sarcastic tone. She knew very well if things did not go according to plan, John L. would take her out. And if not John L., Big Nick would be next in line. Wilma studied both of them carefully. John L. sat there, grinning.

"Can you start Monday?" asked Wilma.

"Yes!" exclaimed Doreetha.

"Excuse me baby, can I talk to John L. for a minute?" asked Wilma nicely.

Doreetha nodded and exited the backroom. Wilma turned serious.

"I need you to get her here on time. And if my register is

off by one penny, she's gone. If she disrespects the clients, she's gone. You hear?"

"Loud and clear," said John L.

John L. got up to leave but Wilma wasn't done lecturing.

"And go to Woolworth's, get her a uniform, white stockings, and some shoes."

"You won't regret this, Wilma."

John L. closed the door behind him. He held Doreetha's hand in the middle of the shop. This took Doreetha off guard because it was an act of intimacy he had never shown her before. As they exited the salon, he pulled her in close.

"We're in, baby," declared John L.

He proceeded to make out with her. Kim was finishing up her cigarette and watched the two go at it. John L. saw Kim in his peripheral vision, which caused him to stop kissing Doreetha. The two approached Kim. He knocked the cigarette out of her hands, almost burning her with it.

"Mind your fucking business, chink."

John L. and Doreetha hopped into John L.'s Cadillac.

Kim contemplated the meaning behind John L.'s comment.

What did "we're in" mean. What was he planning?
thought Kim.

Kim would have addressed her concerns to Wilma that day if Wilma had only taken her side in the argument with Bryce.

Fuck 'em all, I'll have my own business one day, thought Kim.

Chapter 12: 1963 (Part Three)

On Sunday, June 23, 1963 the city of Detroit hosted a

Civil Rights March that drew crowds of 125,000, making it the

largest civil rights demonstration in American history up until the

March on Washington that would take place two months later.

The date was chosen because it was the 20th Anniversary of the

Race Riot that took place in Detroit in 1943, which made some

skeptics contemplate.

What has really changed since then?

The father of future music sensation: Aretha Franklin,

was Reverend Clarence L. Franklin. He along with Reverend

Albert Cleage, Mayor of Detroit: Jerome Cavanaugh, President of

the United Auto Workers: Walter Reuther, and Martin Luther

King Jr. organized and led the historic march. Governor George

Romney was unable to attend because the march conflicted with

his religious practices. He did however send representatives to

walk in his place and show his support. The march began 3pm

that day at the intersection of Woodward Avenue and Adelaide

and lasted an hour and a half. The march ended at Cobo Hall

where Wilma, Ronnie, Ricky, and a throng of 25,000 people were packed into, so they could hear the highly anticipated speeches from the leaders of the march. Wilma was pleased to have heard her friend and business associate, Congressman Charles Diggs speak, but it was the booming voice of Martin Luther King Jr. that won the crowd that day.

"I have a dream this afternoon that one day right here in Detroit, Negroes will be able to buy a house or rent a house anywhere that their money will carry them and they will be able to get a job," declared Reverend King.

Applause erupted and shook the arena. Wilma and Ricky gave King a standing ovation while Ronnie slumped in his chair. Wilma's eyes met with the man sitting next to her. He was a short, muscular man of mid complexion, who Wilma concluded was only a little younger than her. She smiled and checked him out, appreciating how his body shape fit into the tight white shirt he wore. He smiled back at Wilma and decided to start conversation.

"He's a real visionary, isn't he?" shouted the man.

"He really is. An inspiration," said Wilma.

"I'm Fritz."

Ronnie and Ricky turned toward each other both flabbergasted by the obscurity of such a name.

"Fritz?!?" they both exclaimed in unison.

"These are my kids. Ricky and Ronnie."

Fritz was taken aback by Ronnie's chin. He tried to hide his reaction but Ronnie noticed. Fritz extended his hand for a shake. Wilma shook his hand.

"And you are?" he asked.

"Wilma Bailey."

"Are you the owner of Bailey's Salon over on Linwood?"

"Yeah..."

"My friends Ruby and Miranda always praise you. You're like a Goddess to them."

This was the nicest compliment Wilma had received in awhile. She couldn't help but blush, especially since the comment came from someone she was attracted to.

"I just love doing hair," said Wilma simply.

"Not working today?"

"We're closed every Sunday anyway. No way I was gonna miss this. I feel like I'm part of history or something."

Ricky looked at Wilma, annoyed. Any other male giving their attention to his mother always rubbed Ricky the wrong way.

"With this faith, we will be able to achieve this new day when all of God's children, black men and white men, Jews and Gentiles, Protestants and Catholics, will be able to join hands and sing with the Negroes in the spiritual of old: Free at last! Free at last! Thank God almighty, we are free at last!"

Applause erupted again, this time much more loudly. The large crowd got on their feet and clapped. It seemed that everyone gave King praise except Ronnie. As Ronnie grew older, his cynicism grew stronger. He never agreed with King's non-violence approach to Civil Rights. He thought if white men could inflict pain upon the Negroes and get away with it, then Negroes should have that same luxury. Ronnie would not clap for a man who he felt was too "soft" to create any real change. King waved goodbye and walked off the stage. People began to leave the arena. Wilma noticed that Fritz was tearing up. This was the first man she saw cry since she her father did after her mother's death.

"You okay?" asked Wilma sympathetically.

"Yeah. I'm sorry. I just get emotional at these kinds of things. Like I have real hope, you know?"

Ronnie scoffed at the guy but Wilma looked at him glowingly. She realized that a man showing his emotions really turned her on. Barney and Jack were not sensitive but this man was different and Wilma liked it.

"Can I walk out with you?" asked Fritz.

"Of course."

Ronnie and Ricky walked in front of Wilma and Fritz. They inched their way slowly through the sea of people.

"Did you like Dr. King's speech?" asked Fritz to the boys.

Ronnie ignored the man and Ricky nodded. These were typical responses from an eleven and a seven year old.

"I'm hungry, Mama," whined Ronnie.

"How about we all go out for some burgers? My treat." suggested Fritz excitedly.

"That sounds great but could we go to Esquire?" asked Wilma.

"Is that the delicatessen over on Dexter?" asked Fritz.

"Yeah, if that's okay with you."

"I could go for a good corn beef sandwich."

Wilma and Fritz exchanged embarrassing smiles as they exited Cobo Hall.

"What kind of damn name is Fritz?" whispered Ronnie to Ricky.

The Detroit Walk to Freedom that took place in June happened to be a practice demonstration for the March on Washington for Jobs and Freedom in August. There was an atmosphere of intimidation. The Los Angeles Times headquarters was threatened to be destroyed unless they printed an article that called President Kennedy a "Nigger Lover." That morning, five airplanes were grounded because of bomb threats and King was threatened to be assassinated by a caller from Kansas City. Despite all of the threats, the assembly was peaceful and inspirational.

At Wilma's house, she sat next to Fritz on the couch, their hands entwined. They listened intently to a radio broadcast. Using the skills Wilma instilled in him, Ricky made himself a grilled cheese sandwich in a cast iron skillet. Ronnie arranged his green army men toys on the floor of the living room. The reception from the radio had a lot of static but was still audible.

"I have a dream, that my four little children will one day live in a nation where they will not be judged by the color of their skin but by the content of their character. I have a dream today!"

"He used the dream line like he did at Cobo," said Wilma happily.

"It's a good theme. Hopeful, really," said Fritz.

"Now the job is making it a reality," said Wilma.

"I think if we keep marching and stay peaceful, we've got a chance," said Fritz.

It only took two months but Wilma had fallen in love with Fritz. Although he was unemployed, he became a great babysitter for the boys and was the first man she dated that supported her business and independence. He was her cheerleader and her lover at the same time. Fritz's comment earned him a kiss. Ronnie's face turned the same color as his army men, as he turned his body away from them with green envy.

"Ricky, could you get me a glass of ice water, baby."

"Sure, Mama."

Ricky poured a glass of water and put ice in it. He walked over to Wilma and Fritz, slowly. Ronnie studied Ricky's movements and pulled out his leg, subtly. Ricky tripped and spilled the water onto Fritz's shirt.

"Damn it!" yelled Fritz.

"Ricky! What the hell was that? Go get a towel," shouted Wilma.

"Ronnie tripped me, Mama."

Wilma glared at Ronnie. Ricky ran to get a towel from the kitchen. Ronnie proceeded to absolve himself of any wrongdoing, like he always did.

"It wasn't my fault. Ricky doesn't look where he's going."

"You tripped me and you know it!" yelled Ricky.

Ricky handed Wilma a towel and she proceeded to wipe down Fritz's shirt.

"Quiet! Both of you!" yelled Wilma.

"I just had this dry cleaned too," said Fritz.

"It's just water, baby," said Wilma.

"Don't cry over spilled milk, Fritz," said Ronnie with a smirk.

Fritz narrowed his eyes at Ronnie. Fritz had known he was not Ronnie's biggest fan but he did not care. Wilma liked Fritz enough to keep him around and some punk kid was not going to change anything. Fritz could deal with the occasional prank or, in Ronnie's mind "battle," like the hypothetical ones he created with his army men toys. Ronnie may have won a battle but he would ultimately lose the war and the reason was the way Wilma looked at Fritz. A gaze she had not given since she married Jack. Wilma was falling in love and Ronnie could not trip her without Fritz catching her.

November 22, 1963 started out as an ordinary autumn day at Detroit's Brady Elementary School. The sun shined and the leaves fell during recess as Ricky and a bunch of Negro students played "cops and robbers." One black boy snuck up behind a clueless Ricky.

"Bang! You're dead!"

Ricky had avoided being shot during the whole game and right before recess ended, the restless "robber" took him out. The teachers rounded up the students and soon everyone was filing back to the confines of their classroom. Ricky was surprised to see a television set on a cart when he and the rest of the students entered the classroom. Everyone took their seats and stared blankly at the screen. "The most trusted man in America;" Walter Cronkite of CBS, reported from his studio desk. Ricky and his fellow students listened intently.

"There has been an attempt, as perhaps you know now, on the life of President Kennedy. He was wounded in an automobile driving from Dallas Airport into downtown Dallas, along with Governor Connally of Texas, and they've been taken to Parkland Hospital where their condition is as yet unknown."

Ricky thought everyone loved President Kennedy but that

was clearly not true if someone tried to kill him. Ricky was dumbfounded, shocked, and speechless.

Ronnie's reaction was not as intense. He was actually fast asleep with his head on the desk when the news hit. The rest of the students were entranced by the television set and Walter Cronkite's broadcast.

"Regarding the possible assassin, the sheriff's office have taken a young man into custody at the scene, a man 25 years old..." reported Cronkite.

An older Negro teacher with gray hair and a gray mustache, walked up to Ronnie's desk. He swiftly smacked Ronnie on the back of the head with a rolled up newspaper, waking Ronnie up instantly.

"Huh? What's going on?" said Ronnie dazedly.

"History, Ronald. You are sleeping through history," replied the teacher.

Ronnie gazed at the television screen. All he saw was that "boring old white guy from the news." He put his head back down and managed to hear bits and pieces of the broadcast.

When he discovered President Kennedy had been shot at, he quickly raised his head. Although Ronnie did not care for Kennedy or any kind of politics, he could sense a change coming to his neighborhood and the world.

How could this happen? he and millions of people thought.

Big Nick was not one of those millions of people. He may have been surprised when he heard about Kennedy's condition, but he was not about to sit mindlessly in front of a television set and let the event take up real estate in his mind. Then it hit him as he was walking down Jefferson Avenue. In every store window he peered into, everyone was distracted by their television sets, giving him the opportunity to steal when it would be least expected. John L. had told Big Nick to be patient with his "plan" but out of all the traits Big Nick had, patience was not one of them. He was a man of impulsive action and he proved it on that somber afternoon. Big Nick approached the counter of a liquor store, holding his revolver.

"Empty the register, mother fucker!"

The timid old white man slowly opened the register. He hesitated for just enough time for a Beat Cop to walk by and see everything. Another thing Big Nick did not possess was luck. Despite all of the money he made off of his prostitutes, and his impatience with John L., Big Nick let his desire for money blind him of any legal ramifications. He would be sentenced to three years in prison.

Fritz walked through the front door of Wilma's house, carrying two large suitcases. Today was the day he would move in, solidifying the seriousness of their relationship. He noticed Wilma sitting on the couch in the living room. Her mouth was wide open and her skin was pale.

"Baby, shouldn't you be at the shop?"

Wilma did not look at nor reply to Fritz. Her eyes were fixated on the television screen. Fritz dropped his suitcases and without saying a word, sat next to Wilma and watched Walter Cronkite reveal the catastrophic news.

"From Dallas, Texas, the flash apparently official: President Kennedy died at 1:00 p.m. Central Standard Time. 2:00

p.m. Eastern Standard Time, some 38 minutes ago..."

The broadcast continued but was internally drowned out by the collective shock of Wilma and Fritz. They looked into each other's distressed eyes and then held each other. The leader of the free world, a man who looked passed race and fought for Civil Rights, was dead.

If they could kill the President of the United States, then no one is safe, thought Wilma.

Chapter 13: Winter 1966

"No memorial oration or eulogy could more eloquently honor President Kennedy's memory than the earliest possible passage of the Civil Rights bill for which he fought so long."

Although the longevity and passion behind Kennedy's "fight for Civil Rights" was definitely debatable, President Johnson had no trouble using the tragedy of the assassination to play politics in an address to a joint session of Congress five days after Kennedy's death. Congress ended up passing the monumental Civil Rights Act of 1964 but it did not have overwhelming sympathy. After a grueling 75-day filibuster, the Act was passed in the summer of 1964 and a year later the Voting Rights Act of 1965 would be signed into law, prohibiting racial discrimination at the polls. Although these were milestone landmarks for the nation, there was an overall feeling of concern among the African American entrepreneurs of Detroit.

How will this legislation affect our businesses?

Is our clientele here to stay?

Wilma had not yet posed these types of questions as she

rejoiced with her boyfriend in the fact that the dream they heard Martin Luther King Jr. speak of, was becoming a reality. But as the old saying goes; "what goes up, must come down." Three days after the law was passed, a riot erupted in the Watts neighborhood of Los Angeles after police officers racially profiled a Negro driver. After six days of violence, 34 people died, 1,032 were injured, and 3,438 were arrested. Wilma and Fritz's enthusiasm for King's dream waned as they sat and watched the riots unfold on television.

I'm just glad this isn't happening here, thought Wilma.

January of 1966 was a snowy and slow month for the city of Detroit. On an afternoon day, the snow fell like rain. Cars moved like snails on the white streets of Linwood. The red painted letters of "Bailey's Salon" on the front window was barely visible. Inside the salon there were no clients. At the front desk, sat Doreetha who had been perched there for the past three years as Wilma's receptionist and main runner of the numbers. In those three years she and Wilma formed a friendship. Wilma had a certain level of trust in Doreetha, which she never thought she would have for a prostitute. John L. had certainly given her an opportunity for a better life, which at times confused Wilma, because he had given up his "best girl" as a source of income. Wilma's gratefulness outweighed her confusion. Luckily there were no demanding responsibilities that day, for Doreetha was bobbing her head and drifting in and out of consciousness. Seated at her own station was Janette who was in her own world reading a newspaper. Bryce filed his nails and rocked back and forth in his squeaky salon chair. Bryce's vision shifted from his nails through the open backroom door to Kim, who stuffed her face with a Korean noodle dish. It was a dish heavy in garlic and sesame seed oil. Bryce sliced the silence with his sharp tone.

"Is no one gonna say nothin'?" blurted Bryce.

Everyone remained silent and simply stared at Bryce. Doreetha now had a reason to stay awake as she sensed drama was about to be dispersed. Kim kept eating, oblivious of Bryce's comment.

"Now I know why Wilma keeps you in the backroom. Your food stink!" said Bryce.

"Your breath stink," retorted Kim.

Janette and Doreetha chuckled loudly. The slow snowy day just got interesting. As someone who always craved to be the center of attention, Bryce hated when other people made jokes, especially if they were at his expense. The laughter that emanated from the ladies fueled an angry fire in Bryce that made spewing his next comment all the more easy.

"Why don't you go back to Korea? No one wants you here."

Kim stopped eating and stared at Bryce. Her English wasn't the best but she understood that loud and clear.

"Bryce!" yelled Janette, offended by Bryce's rudeness.

"Come on, Janette. You know she steals our supplies," said Bryce.

Janette had in fact suspected Kim of taking a pair of scissors from her new kit after Kim meandered by her station a few weeks back. This thought prevented Janette from any further defense of Kim. Wilma walked into the salon, only to find Kim throwing her food in the garbage forcefully.

"I quit," stated Kim as she looked into Wilma's eyes.

This can't be happening. No one makes and styles wigs like Kim, thought Wilma.

Kim ran into in the backroom. She proceeded to throw all of her supplies into her large handbag swiftly and then rushed toward the exit.

"Kim, we can talk this out," said Wilma.

"No. No hope. I leave," said Kim flatly.

"Heading back to the motherland?" asked Bryce sarcastically.

Kim gave Bryce the middle finger and left the salon in a huff. As the door opened, snow fluttered in and a gust of wind chilled everyone to the bone before the door shut on its own. Wilma turned to Bryce infuriately.

"If another employee or client leaves this shop because of you, you can walk right out behind them. You understand?"

Bryce never saw Wilma this angry. He nodded slowly, afraid that he might be the next one leaving the salon. The phone rang loudly which gave Bryce a whole new appreciation for the term: "saved by the bell." Wilma's attention turned to Doreetha as she picked up the phone.

"Thank you for calling Bailey's Salon, would you like to make an appointment?"

Doreetha listened for a few seconds before responding.

"One moment please."

Wilma walked closer to the counter with a curious look on her face.

"It's Congressman Diggs for you," said Doreetha.

Wilma smiled and took the receiver from Doreetha.

"Hey, Charlie," said Wilma pleasantly.

Wilma respected Diggs for his public service and Diggs admired Wilma for her work ethic. They were good friends who had not talked in years. In fact, it was when Martin Luther King Jr. spoke at Cobo was when Wilma last saw Diggs in the flesh. His funeral home was run by competent associates so this was the first conversation she had with the Congressman in a long time. After Kim quitting, it was refreshing to talk to an old friend but Digg's tone was not his usual upbeat kind. He reminded Wilma of a business meeting for Negro business owners. Wilma hated these meeting but this particular one would be a necessity. Business wasn't what it used to be and Wilma hoped that going to this meeting would give her some hope for the future.

The snow had stopped falling but it was a bitter night in Detroit. Wilma was bundled up like an Eskimo as she walked down the sidewalk briskly. She watched as a cigarette butt was flicked onto the pavement, almost searing her left shoe. She stopped to confront the figure that almost lit her shoelaces on fire, only to make eye contact with her dear old friend. Any attempt at arson was instantly forgiven.

"Charlie!" said Wilma.

Congressman Diggs smiled and hugged Wilma. He was dressed to impress with his black suit and stripped tie sticking out of his black overcoat.

"Thanks again for reminding me about this meeting," said Wilma.

"Can't leave out one of Detroit's most successful business owners," responded Diggs.

Even in the arctic atmosphere, Wilma was still able to blush. Diggs put his arm around her and they walked together toward their destination.

"Well, you're not doing bad yourself. How's the funeral home going?" asked Wilma.

"It's going well. But between the Civil Rights Act and Voting Rights Act, our clientele is leaving the city," said Diggs with an ominous tone.

"I hope this meeting helps both our businesses."

"I just don't understand why we're leaving our city. The Jews and the Italians didn't leave their towns. Why the hell should we?"

They walked passed a sign that read: "Booker T. Washington Business Association" and escalated the stairs of the brown building. Wilma and Congressman Diggs entered an auditorium filled with over one hundred middle-aged Negroes. Some socialized but most sat in their seats and waited patiently for the meeting to start. Wilma glanced at one Negro man who was walking toward her. He had a bushy mustache and a nappy fro that made Wilma cringe. He made eye contact with Wilma, yet extended his hand to Congressman Diggs.

"Mr. Diggs, Curtis Davenport. It's a pleasure to finally meet you in person," said Curtis loudly over the commotion.

Diggs and Curtis shook hands as Wilma took in the setting.

"I'm from Mississippi and I just wanted to say that what you did for Emmett Till's family was touching," said Curtis sincerely.

"Thank you. I think if we had the trial today, it would have been a different verdict."

"I don't know about that."

"Mississippi you say? What brings you so far up north?"

"Same as everyone else. Came up to make cars."

More people noticed Diggs by the entrance and made their way towards him, pushing Wilma to the periphery of the crowd. An isolated Wilma walked to the end of a middle row and sat in a chair. She was impressed with the turnout. Usually only half of today's crowd would come.

I guess desperate times call for desperate measures. After all, it is partially desperation why I go to these things. Silverman can bring in the gamblers but not the colored women looking for a good styling, thought Wilma.

Wilma's trend of thought was interrupted by ten middle-aged Negro men walking onto the front stage. The gentlemen took their assigned seats. Chairman Hill wore a long black beard and sat in the middle of the line of board members. He spoke into the microphone placed on the table in front of him and his booming voice was projected into the echoing auditorium.

"Hello everyone. Welcome to our Economic and Community Committee Meeting. If you could please take your seats, we can begin."

The chattering subsided and everyone took their seats.

"Before the Board outlines our agenda, I think we should open up the panel to all of you; the entrepreneurs of Detroit. This is our biggest turnout, after all," declared Chairman Hill.

About a fourth of the attendees raised their hands, including Wilma. Chairman Hill pointed to James who sat in the front row with his hand held high.

"Please state your name and your business," said Chairman Hill.

A microphone was handed to James and he spoke into it anxiously.

"My name is James. I manage the Avalon Theater on Linwood."

"And why are you here, James?" inquired Hill.

"The same reason everyone else is. We're all hurting because our customers are moving to the suburbs."

The crowd resumed their chattering, prompting Chairman Hill to bang his gavel and demand order and silence. Seated between James and Wilma was Martha Jean "The Queen," an attractive Negro woman who was as light-skinned as Wilma. Wilma could not help but admire her hair, which was set perfectly. "The Queen" stood up haughtily and made her presence known.

"I'm Martha Jean but everyone knows who I am."

"We all know, Queen. Go on," said Chairman Hill.

Like Wilma, Martha Jean "The Queen" had moved to Detroit from her rural homeland to market her creative talents. For Wilma, it was doing hair and for "The Queen," it was being a radio broadcaster. She had a smooth and a calming voice that transitioned through all types of Jazz songs seamlessly on Detroit's new FM network: WJLB.

"I don't understand why you are upset about people leaving. We now have equal opportunities to live wherever we want."

"We don't have to move. We need to invest in our city and in ourselves and that will create a greater tax base and a larger consumer market," chimed in James.

The chattering became louder in that moment. Martha Jean shook her head and sat back down. She had no intention on fighting any debates. Her main priority was remaining "well liked" by her constituents for her own job security.

"Thank you, James. Everyone please settle down," stated Chairman Hill.

Chairman Hill banged his gavel and pointed to Coleman

Young, a light-skinned Negro man, who wore an Afro and glasses.

"I'm Coleman Young of Young's Barbecue and I'm only getting business on the weekends when people are on their way to Bell Isle. What am I supposed to do during the week? Starve?"

Young tended to have a flair for the dramatic, but his point was valid. He was only getting weekend traffic to his restaurant and that would not pay the bills. Although this meeting was structured around finding solutions and working together, Wilma noticed that it was also a place to vent which made one feel a little bit better even if answers could not be found.

"That's why we're here, Coleman. We're trying to figure this out," said Chairman Hill.

Chairman Hill then pointed to Wilma, who still had her hand up. Before she could get a word out, a nearby Negro man named, Franklin interjected rudely.

"Hey! Wait a minute! My hand was up first!"

"Okay, Franklin. State your business," said Chairman Hill.

"You know I'm the owner of Checker's Barbecue and I don't know why Wilma has her hand up, everyone know she's doing good anyway," said Franklin.

Coleman Young thought Franklin was going to talk down his fried chicken and could not help but smile when that was not the case. Wilma was flabbergasted. Not only had the guy interrupted her, he diminished her problems out of some form of jealousy or resentment. Wilma turned to Franklin, not letting him get away with it.

"I beg your pardon, *Frank*. But because of the Afros, I've lost fifty percent of my business. All I got now are old ladies. If I lose them, I'm done."

It was that simple. People were not getting their hair done like they used to. After the empowerment of Civil Rights and the mass suburbanization, Wilma was not getting the clients like she used to. Coleman Young had met Wilma a few times and knew Mr. Silverman. His knowledge of Wilma's business arrangement prompted him to blurt out his next comment that tended to add more tension to the meeting rather than constructive commentary.

"The Jews and the Italians are in our pocket. Our clientele is leaving the city. What in God's name are we going to do?"

The crowd chatter was at its loudest. Wilma sat down and reflected on Coleman's statement.

Mr. Silverman was technically in my pocket. But it's still my business. I'm in control, thought Wilma.

The crowd, however, was going out of control as Chairman Hill banged the gavel continuously to try and calm down a multitude of entrepreneurs that feared for their businesses, families, and their livelihoods.

The Negro entrepreneurs were not the only ones concerned about their investments. That same night Mr. Silverman entered Silverman's Cleaners with a slight nervousness of what *his* boss had to say. The Union President: Mr. Hoffman liked every meeting set to a certain schedule which made this evening's "impromptu meeting" a bit nerve-racking. Moe followed dutifully behind Mr. Silverman as they entered the office. Seated at Silverman's large black desk was Mr. Hoffman. He was a middle-aged white man with graying black hair slicked back. He had a suit on and his wing tip shoes were placed on the desk next to a sign that read: "Mr. Silverman: Manager."

"You're in my chair," said Mr. Silverman.

"Union Presidents have that liberty, Max. Sit down, gentlemen" said Mr. Hoffman.

Mr. Silverman and Moe sat on chairs positioned in front of the desk. Mr. Silverman shifted his perspective to that of one of his employees when they would sit and face the boss. He hated it as much as he hated being called Max, but Mr. Silverman knew his place and it was under Hoffman.

"Got any nigger neighbors yet?" asked Mr. Hoffman.

"If it wasn't for Humphrey and that fuckin' filibuster, Civil Rights would have never passed," said Moe fumingly.

"It wasn't all that bad," said Mr. Silverman.

"Max, you've always had a soft spot for them, huh?" blurted Mr. Hoffman.

"We still got our policy," said Mr. Silverman.

"Not for long. You've been to Bailey's. The place is dead. The city has highest income per capita and the niggers are fuckin' leaving," said Moe.

"Well, maybe if we sell them the houses instead of renting, maybe they'll stay," said Mr. Silverman.

"It's too late for that. The fuckin' eggplants are stupid. Detroit has the highest GDP and they want to come live next door to us. What a fucking joke," said Mr. Hoffman.

Mr. Hoffman lit his cigar and inhaled deeply. Watching this inspired Mr. Silverman to light one of his cigarettes. All this complaining seemed like it was going to be an unproductive meeting. That was until Mr. Hoffman brought up a new entrepreneurial vision for Detroit.

"But have no fear, gentlemen. Revenue is about to go sky high."

Moe and Mr. Silverman looked at him skeptically.

"Our brave men in uniform risked their lives to bring us this gift and we need all the fuckers we have left to spread the love," declared Mr. Hoffman.

Mr. Hoffman pulled out a large brown bag from under his feet and placed it on the desk. Moe stood up and opened it. His eyes bulged at the sight of what was inside.

"Smack?" inquired Moe surprisingly.

"The purest there is," said Mr. Hoffman.

"This is our ace in the hole," said Moe with a sense of wonder and excitement.

Mr. Silverman did not see it as an "ace in the hole" but more of a liability and a danger.

"Do we really want this shit in our streets? What about the kids? What about our kids?" asked Mr. Silverman.

"Don't worry about it. We'll keep it in the Negro neighborhoods," said Mr. Hoffman gravely.

Moe nodded approvingly. Mr. Silverman was not the biggest activist for Civil Rights, but he coexisted peacefully with the Negroes and hated to see this drug infect their communities. All he saw coming out of this was destruction and it would not be worth the profit. But Mr. Silverman was not one to fight for what he believed in from a moral standpoint. He had to make his own living just like the struggling black entrepreneurs.

"Time to start recruiting!" said Mr. Hoffman.

Mr. Hoffman extinguished his cigar in the ashtray next to the bag of heroin. For a split second, Mr. Silverman hoped that the bag would catch fire and put Mr. Hoffman's "pipe dream" up in smoke. Mr. Silverman grew up in Detroit and saw what drugs had done to his friends and family. He thought that he would never place that fate on anyone no matter what color their skin was. Mr. Hoffman and Moe did not share Mr. Silverman's idealism and sympathy but neither did Mr. Silverman, full heartedly anyway. He kept his mouth shut. Business was business but Detroit would never be the same again.

A few days later, Wilma and Fritz sat in the dining area at their favorite delicatessen; Esquire. The restaurant was filled with all Negroes, most of them wearing Afros. A Negro woman with a large Afro walked passed the seated couple. Wilma stared at her hair angrily, thinking of all the possible styles she could do with such a "frizz ball." Fritz could not help but notice her glare.

"Thanks for lunch, baby," said Fritz.

"I have to lay off half my staff. Everyone's wearing Afros. People are moving to the suburbs. There's talk of Motown going out west..."

Wilma started hyperventilating. She felt as if she was sinking to the bottom of the ocean with concrete blocks from the foundation of her business tied to her legs. She was drowning in that moment. Drowning in her own pessimistic thoughts.

"Wilma, breathe," said Fritz calmly.

The smoothness and tranquility of Fritz's voice was her oxygen mask. Wilma took a deep breath and exhaled.

"You still got the Diggs and Swanson accounts and plenty of clients."

"I still got the numbers," said Wilma dazedly.

"And don't worry the Afro is just a fad."

Wilma shook her head to snap out of her mini panic attack. She studied her menu while Fritz had already closed his, confident in his delicious decision. Wilma could not focus on the menu when thoughts of Ricky and Ronnie were the next synapses that fired in her brain.

"This was all for my sons. So they have a better life."

Fritz placed his hand on Wilma's. He looked at her and

waited until she made eye contact with him before he spoke.

"Wilma, don't worry. I got your back. I'll take care of the boys, you take care of the business."

Fritz was more than her oxygen mask. He was her life preserver. Never before had she felt such a strong connection to a man. Barney cared more about alcohol than he did his own wife and child. Jack cared more about money than his own wife and child. But Fritz cared more for Wilma and children that weren't even his more than Barney and Jack combined. Wilma fell deeper in love with Fritz after he said that.

What man would be willing to sacrifice a job and stay at home to watch kids that weren't even his and ask for nothing in return? Fritz was one of a kind. A great catch, thought Wilma.

"That's all I need you to do. Don't worry about any job. Just take care of the kids," said Wilma.

"Okay, baby," said Fritz.

Wilma smiled for the first time that day. A short, white waiter, wearing glasses and his own Afro, arrived at the table.

"What can I get you two?" the waiter asked nasally.

Wilma hesitated and finally looked over her menu again. Her eyes moved back and forth quickly like windshield wipers in a rainstorm. Fritz's initial plan was to embrace the "ladies first" ideology but Wilma took too long for Fritz's patience.

"I'll--" said Wilma briefly.

"I'll have the smoked white fish with coleslaw and cheesecake for dessert," interrupted Fritz with a decisive tone.

"Um...Pastrami is fine," said Wilma distraughtly.

Although Fritz was a blessing to Wilma in many ways, it still bothered her that he rarely offered to pay for anything. She knew he did not have a job but he did talk about an inheritance he had gotten from his uncle. He only brought it up once and never did again.

Jack used to buy me things and take me out... but Fritz is here for me. Jack wasn't. It's not all about money. I love Fritz and he loves me, thought Wilma.

Chapter 14: Spring 1966

A few months had passed and the snow had finally melted. The Detroit Redwings had just lost the Stanley Cup to the Montreal Canadiens. Although hockey was not particularly popular among the Negro community, entrepreneurs made good money that was shared cheerfully at The 20 Grand Club that night. John L., looking as debonair as ever, entered the club wearing a black and red sharkskin suit. He walked passed the attractive waitresses and checked all of them out. Dollar amounts swarmed in his head regarding what he could make off of each one. He approached a table booth where Big Nick was seated, wearing a bright green suit and standing out from the crowd. He had a girl on each arm and wore the biggest grin on his face.

"Looks like you're back in the swing of things," said John L.

Big Nick's grin quickly faded as his eyes met with John L.'s Big Nick moved his arms off of the ladies and put them on the table.

"Go dance," said Big Nick flatly.

Although his eyes remained on John L., the girls knew the order was for them. Both girls stood up and sauntered to the dance floor.

"They didn't look me in the eye. You built loyalty fast," said John L.

John L. pulled a chair from a nearby table and sat down across from Big Nick.

"And I thought I owned every working girl in this city," continued John L.

"Things change," said Big Nick bluntly.

John L. studied his surroundings. He noticed people in the club glancing at Big Nick and then quickly looking away in fear.

"It's funny how much a prison sentence can earn you more respect," said John L.

"What do you want, Johnny boy?"

"To finish where we left off before you got your ass locked up."

"What the fuck are you talking about?"

"The pieces are in place, Nick. The pots gotten a lot

bigger since you've been gone."

"What the fuck do you want, man?"

"Your reputation."

John L.'s attention shifted from Big Nick to a figure in the corner of the club. John L. tilted his head to the side and squinted his eyes in disbelief as he peered across the club. He stood up abruptly, almost knocking Big Nick's drink off the table.

"What the fuck, man?" asked Big Nick.

"Who the fuck is he talking to? Nick, I gotta go see what this motherfuckers doing. I'll call you later."

Later that day, Bailey's Salon was unusually slow. Wilma thought there would be more traffic once the snow thawed but spring of 1966 was not as lively as previous springs before. That notion was reflected through Doreetha as she slouched at the counter. Janette swept up the fallen hair of her previous client. Wilma curled the long gray hair of Miss Cobb. Miss Cobb was Wilma's oldest client and also her nicest. Cobb challenged the stereotype that all old people were grumpy. Even though business was slow, Miss Cobb made the atmosphere of the shop more upbeat. As Wilma finished, they both looked in the mirror.

"How does that look, Miss Cobb?"

"It's perfect."

Wilma smiled and took off her apron. She turned Miss Cobb's salon chair to face the front and began to put some supplies away.

"You've got talent, Wilma. You must love doing hair."

"I do."

Miss Cobb grabbed Wilma's hand. This took Wilma aback, mostly because of how fast the old lady moved her hand.

"If there's anything I've learned all these years it's that you should never let anyone stop you from doing what you love," said Miss Cobb sincerely.

John L. opened the door quickly, which caused the entrance bell to fall to the floor. He looked at Doreetha then at Wilma with a seriousness both women had never seen.

"Wilma, you need to come with me right now," said John L. assertively.

"John L., I'm with a client."

Miss Cobb made eye contact with John L. in the mirror. She looked down nervously, getting a bad vibe from John L.'s demeanor.

"Something's going on at your house," said John L.

"What?" inquired Wilma incredulously.

"It's something you need to see."

A disconcerted Wilma stared at John L. and decided that more questions would not address her concerns as much as seeing what John L. wanted her to see would. She hated leaving the shop early, but since business was slow and John L. was concerned, Wilma made an exception.

"Janette, can you please finish up with Miss Cobb and watch the shop?"

Janette had overheard everything. If she were in Wilma's position, she would have already been on her way home. She understood the urgency of the situation.

"Of course, Wilma. Go."

"I'm sorry Miss Cobb, I have to go but Janette will check you out," said Wilma.

Miss Cobb nodded hesitantly. She did not trust John L. but she trusted Wilma's judgment. Wilma and John L. left the shop and took John L.'s car. During the whole ride, John L. refused to say what was going on at the house. He stayed silent.

Whatever is going on, I'm just glad Ronnie and Ricky are at school, thought Wilma.

John L. parked outside Wilma's house. Wilma got out quickly and walked briskly to the front door. John L. followed behind. Visually, everything seemed to be in its rightful place but what Wilma heard in that moment was something that should not be happening in her home. The sounds of loud male moans permeated the house. Wilma's face dropped when she recognized a moan. It was a moan she heard before. Wilma followed the sounds toward her bedroom. John L. was still behind her but both were silent. Wilma opened her bedroom quickly and saw something she would never forget; a naked Negro man thrusting himself in and out of Fritz, who was on his hands and knees.

"What the fuck?" exclaimed the naked man.

He swiftly pulled himself off of Fritz and grabbed his clothes. He rushed out the window and went down the fire escape. Fritz made eye contact with a pale and motionless Wilma.

"Oh my God, Wilma!"

A naked Fritz jumped out of bed and ran towards Wilma. Wilma sprinted out, knowing she never wanted to see him again. Fritz attempted to follow her, but John L. stood in his way.

"Wait a minute!" yelled Fritz.

John L. smiled and cracked him over the forehead with his 38 Police Special. Fritz fell to the floor as blood began to gush from his head. John L. kicked him in the face and then three times in the chest. Blood splattered onto the carpet. Fritz lay there, sprawled out naked and bleeding. His moans were now definitely less pleasurable.

"Now get the fuck out, fag. And don't ever come back."

Fritz tried to stand up but fell back to the floor. John L. grabbed his arm and dragged him down the hallway and out the front door. Fritz's naked body was laid out on the sidewalk next to Wilma, who chose to ignore him. John L. came out and threw Fritz's clothes on top of him.

"If you come back, I'll blow your fucking head off," said John L. devilishly.

Fritz managed to stand and covered his private parts with his clothes. With a bloody face and tears in his eyes, he looked at Wilma. Wilma refused to make eye contact. Her back was turned away from him.

"I'm sorry, Wilma," said Fritz somberly.

"Get the fuck out of here," yelled John L.

Fritz puckered his face and hobbled into an alley. John L. approached Wilma and hugged her. For the first time in a long time, Wilma Bailey cried. The man she loved more than anyone, probably never loved her at all. He was not who she thought he was. Her heart was broken and her soul was crushed.

"Don't cry, Wilma. Everything is gonna be all right." Wilma realized that John L.'s words of encouragement were the same words she used to make people feel better. She could not believe those words though. She did not think everything was going to be all right.

The love of my life is gay, my business is failing, and I'm in bed with the mob, thought Wilma anxiously.

Wilma began to breathe heavily and felt like she was drowning again. This time the life preserver that was Fritz was swept away. All Wilma could think of in that moment was Fritz's comment in Esquire.

"Wilma, don't worry. I got your back. I'll take care of the boys; you take care of the business.

Wilma hyperventilated. John L. held her close, hoping his embrace would calm her down.

"Oh my god. Do you think he ever touched my boys?"

"I doubt it, Wilma but I'll talk to Ricky and Ronnie."

Wilma jolted back out of John L.'s arms. She then composed herself.

"No. I'll handle it."

The thought of John L. having such a conversation with her boys, disturbed her. He could barely relate to kids as it was, let alone talk about something so sensitive and scarring. Wilma was no longer mentally drowning. She did not need Fritz as a life preserver when she had two sailors pulling her back in all along:

Ricky and Ronnie.

"Why don't you go inside and lay down? From now on Doreetha can take care of the boys at home while you're at work," said John L.

"That would be fine," said Wilma in a daze.

"She can take the numbers at home now. Make it easier on you."

"I am sick of people coming to my shop just for the numbers."

"Get some rest, Wilma."

John L. kissed Wilma on the cheek and walked to his car. He smirked as he drove off which made Wilma uneasy. In her world there was nothing to smirk about. Wilma went inside and saw that the house was a mess from the recent fiasco. Clothes were scattered over the house and a broken lamp was on the blood stained carpet. Wilma walked into her bedroom and stared at her mattress for a few seconds. She ran to it and ripped it off of the bed frame. She dragged it down the hallway and out the front door. She threw it on the curb where the garbage collectors would dispose of it. Wilma spit on the mattress and went back inside.

Later that day, Ronnie and Ricky came home after school. As they walked in through the front door, they saw something they had not seen since Jack lived with them. It was a half empty bottle of Seagram's Gin placed on the living room table.

"Mama?" inquired Ricky nervously.

All the boys heard was a scrubbing noise that originated from the kitchen. Ronnie and Ricky slowly walked into the kitchen, not knowing what to expect. They found their mother anxiously scrubbing the floor with a rag. It was unlike their mother to have her hair disheveled, let alone, have alcohol out in the open. Wilma looked up at her concerned sons.

"Hey kids! How was school?" asked Wilma enthusiastically.

Wilma stood up and hugged both Ricky and Ronnie at once, squeezing tighter than usual.

"Are you okay, Mama?" asked Ronnie.

"Of course I am. This place is just such a mess. Can you boys help me clean?"

Ricky and Ronnie both looked at each other surprisingly. Although they had no desire to clean, this was the nicest manner in which their mother asked them to do something. They decided to return her niceness with cooperation.

"Sure," said Ronnie as Ricky nodded.

"I love both of you, so much!" said Wilma.

She kissed both of them on their foreheads. Although Ricky and Ronnie appreciated the affection she was giving them, they both knew it was not worth the price of her drinking.

What happened to make her start drinking? thought Ronnie.

Why is Mama drinking? thought Ricky.

"You both finish the dishes. I'll take care of the living room."

Wilma walked to the living room. She began rearranging furniture and throwing out debris. She looked back to see that her sons were out of sight and she took a swig from the bottle.

"Where's Fritz?" yelled Ronnie from the kitchen.

Wilma coughed on her drink as the gin went down the

"wrong pipe." After some coughing and heavy breathing, she answered her son's question vaguely.

"He's gone. You won't see him again."

"Why?" shouted Ricky.

Wilma could never tell her sons the truth. It was too much for them to handle. It was too much for *her* to handle. She knew Ricky and Ronnie well enough to know that if Fritz had done anything inappropriate to them, she would know about it right away. She decided in that moment to assume that Fritz fooled them as well as he fooled her. She also decided to lie to her sons.

"He got a job...out of town."

Ricky turned to Ronnie with a big smirk on his chubby little face.

"Gimme five on the black hand side," said Ricky.

Ricky and Ronnie performed their ritual of excitement. They gave each other "five" in which they smacked together their palms and then their backhands. Fritz, the guy with the weird name, smelly cologne, and who always hogged the television set, was gone. It was not a moment too soon. Wilma watched her son's praises of Fritz's exodus and managed to smile.

At least they are not heartbroken that Fritz is gone. I

yearn for that feeling, thought Wilma.

Chapter 15: Summer 1966

Many Americans were tired of what seemed to be an endless bloodbath in Vietnam. The soldiers returning home to Detroit brought back more than just their baggage, but a monkey on their back. A monkey that was dangerous and unpredictable. A change was coming, one that would transform not just the landscape of Detroit, but the entire nation.

That summer, Wilma Bailey found solace at the bottom of the bottle and became a frequent guest at Chubby's After Hour Joint. Her nights were spent dancing with Shirley and her friends. Shirley embraced the new Wilma with open arms for finally coming out of her shell and having a good time. Although Wilma swore off serious relationships with men, it did not stop her from flirting and dancing with the Negro officer Lester. He may have lost her to Jack years ago, but now he convinced himself that he "won." Although he was infatuated with her, Lester would never be more to Wilma than a drunken distraction.

Unfortunately, Wilma's alcohol did not just stay at home or at the bar. Now that Doreetha spent the summer watching

Ricky and Ronnie at the house, Wilma spent her work days at the front counter, sneakily taking sips from her flask in between paperwork. It was on one of these days that Wilma handed Moe a bag of hair supplies instead of the bag that contained Silverman's cut of the number money. In Wilma's defense, the bags were aesthetically similar.

Throughout the summer, Wilma managed to keep her drinking during business hours a secret from her staff. All the clients and staff members were oblivious, except Bryce. He caught Wilma sneaking a shot once while she was at the counter. Bryce decided to keep his mouth shut in case the information could be used in his favor down the line.

With Wilma drinking everyday, Doreetha would record the policy numbers more competently from the comfort of Wilma's house. In addition to making sure Ricky and Ronnie were fed and looked after, Doreetha's day consisted of taking many phone calls and front door visitors, inundating her with a slew of three number combinations for the daily horse race bets. She recorded everything in her large, hard covered notebook;

generously given to her, as a gift from John L. John L. would often stop by between pimping to make sure Doreetha was doing her job.

Ricky and Ronnie were not bothered by Doreetha's dealings because they were too busy playing and taking care of their new addition to the family; a black poodle they named: Blackie. Wilma used to be against having a dog until one of Ronnie's teachers told her about his obsession with animals. Ronnie would spend most of his recesses at the school aquarium, which did not bode well for his social life. Wilma's logic was to get Ronnie a dog so he could get his animal fix at home and open him up socially at school. The opposite happened.

Ronnie became even more inclusive after his fixation with animals was now out in the open. He spent even more time at the aquarium, simply watching the animals. One girl who shared Ronnie's interest in animals was Sheelah. She also shared his age at 14. The month before school ended, Sheelah and Ronnie would spend everyday at the aquarium, talking about different animals. She was the first girl to see Ronnie's personality and not his disfigured face. Sheelah became Ronnie's first love.

On a blazing summer day, a chubby Ricky, who was now ten years old, walked Blackie down the street. Blackie sniffed the grass around him and was pulled back on the leash when he started to move faster than Ricky.

"Hurry up and doo doo, Blackie."

Ricky accidentally dropped the leash and Blackie darted through someone's freshly cut lawn and went behind a series of houses.

"Blackie! Get your ass back here!" yelled Ricky.

Ricky ran after him as fast as he could. Blackie made his way over to a red shed and proceeded to sniff under the door crack. A panting Ricky approached the shed.

"Blackie, whatcha doin'?"

Blackie began to scratch the bottom of the shed door. Ricky had never seen Blackie this persistent before, piquing his own curiosity. He noticed there was not a lock on the shed door and decided to open it. Blackie rocketed in and started licking Ronnie's leg as he pushed his naked body up against a naked

Sheelah, who was bent over a lawnmower. Her pleasurable moaning quickly turned into a frightened scream as she locked eyes with Ricky.

"Blackie? Ricky? What the fuck? Get outta here! Close the door!" yelled Ronnie.

Ronnie gently nudged Blackie out of the shed as Ricky stared motionless in amazement and wonder.

"But Ronnie...I want some."

Ronnie slammed the shed door in his Ricky's face. Ricky stumbled back and tripped on Blackie's leash, falling straight onto his ass. Ricky managed to hear Sheelah whisper loudly.

"Ron, I don't want him telling anybody. My parents would kill me."

Blackie licked Ricky's face before he got up. A fuming Ricky grabbed Blackie's leash and stormed back home. He entered the house and tiptoed into Wilma's bedroom. Doreetha was sprawled out on the bed, taking a nap. Ricky quietly opened a drawer in Wilma's dresser. He sifted through a bunch white bras and pulled out a few one-dollar bills. He smirked as he stuffed his newfound treasure into his front pocket. His next step was to hail a cab.

It was a good day at Bailey's Salon. The shop was full of clients and stylists alike. "My Baby" by The Temptations played in the background, adding to the already upbeat atmosphere. Wilma, Bryce, Janette, Kathy, and Anita all styled the hair of their respective middle-aged and elderly Negro women clients. Ricky walked in after his cab ride with a pouting face.

"Hey, Ricky," said Bryce.

"Do the dance, Ricky," said Kathy.

"Yeah! Do the twist!" exclaimed Anita.

The clients and the stylists all got kicks out of Ricky's dancing. Ricky ignored everyone's comments and walked straight up to Wilma as she styled.

"What's wrong, baby? Where's Doreetha?" asked Wilma in a motherly manner.

"Mama, I need to talk to you."

Ricky looked at Wilma's client and then at her, which insinuated that Ricky preferred a more private discussion. Wilma turned to her client.

"Excuse me for a second."

Wilma bent down to listen to Ricky as they moved to the center of the shop. Ricky mumbled something into her ear.

"What?" asked Wilma, barely holding back her laughter.

Wilma's loud and quick reaction made Ricky jump. Everyone in the salon was now looking at Wilma and Ricky. Wilma stood up.

"Hey! Hold up! Turn the music down! Be quiet," shouted Wilma.

Anita complied and turned down the jukebox until it was barely audible. Wilma turned to Ricky to hear him again but she wanted his comment to be made public.

"Baby, what happened?"

A pin could drop in that shop and people would hear it. Like Wilma had when she was younger, Ricky had stage fright. He hesitated for a few seconds, knowing that one of the words may be considered a bad word. As the dutiful son he was, he listened to his mother.

"I saw Ronnie doing the pussy!" stated Ricky tearfully.

The shop exploded in laughter, leaving only a few elderly women clients shaking their heads in disapproval. Tears began to stream down Ricky's face. With this being the most attention he ever had in his life, Ricky took the laughter as him being offensive, more so than funny. Wilma bent back down to Ricky, reaching into her apron pocket. She pulled out a one-dollar bill.

"Here's a dollar for you to get some burgers and come back and eat lunch. And don't worry baby, I'm gonna whoop his butt."

Ricky took the money and his sobbing subsided. Wilma wiped away his tears and kissed him on the forehead. Anita took it upon herself to turn the jukebox back up. The Temptations blasted once again and everyone returned to their business. Ricky left that shop with an appetite not for burgers, but for what Ronnie was having.

Later that day, Ronnie made a point to ignore Ricky when he got home. He was angry that his younger brother interrupted such a milestone moment and most likely went off to tell Mama about it. Ronnie did not want to risk talking about the subject while Doreetha was still in the house. She was Wilma's "eyes and ears" after all. He decided to take his frustration out on his bongos that he played loudly and used to retreat from reality. Ricky thought it would be best to keep his distance from his brother, knowing that punishment would soon befall upon him once their mother got home. He sought refuge in the backyard to play with Blackie. This time Blackie was tied to a post to avoid him running off and finding more elicit activities.

He should be a police dog, thought Ricky.

Blackie barked at the sight of a new visitor that just set foot on the lawn. Sheelah slowly approached Ricky with a face that said "innocent school girl" but Ricky knew better.

"Come on," said Sheelah.

Sheelah grabbed Ricky's hand and led him away from his yard. Blackie was too distracted to notice Ricky's departure. A nearby squirrel needed to be chased, although, the effort was futile once the critter climbed up a tree.

Sheelah and Ricky spent five long minutes in the same

shed in which he found her and Ronnie. They exited the shed and began walking back to Ricky's house.

"How did it feel?" asked Sheelah.

"It was warm," replied Ricky smugly.

"You won't tell on me and Ronnie now, right?"

"I won't."

"Good."

Ricky did what some guys twice his age had not experienced yet. After the act, he recognized that fact and was fearful that he did something wrong and knew that he could never tell anyone about it, especially Ronnie. All he could hope for was that his mother did not feel the need to talk to Sheelah's parents. With her drinking, Ricky's mother had become less predictable in the last year. Anything was possible. But one thing was for sure. Ricky had sex and was not proud of it.

That same night, Ricky sat on the couch and watched *The Lucy Show* on the television. Ricky had found the show mildly humorous. When Ronnie entered the room, Ricky stopped laughing which was a cue to Ronnie that something was up.

Doreetha was on the phone and Wilma had not yet arrived. It was Ronnie's opportune moment to confront his younger brother.

"You didn't tell Mama, did you?" asked Ronnie assertively.

Ricky looked at his brother and then snickered to himself.

"Ricky!" Ronnie yelled.

Just as Ronnie was about to lunge at Ricky, the front door swung open, abruptly. Wilma entered but almost tripped on the slight incline between the stoop and the front door. Ronnie composed himself.

"How was work, Mama?"

Wilma slowly walked toward Ronnie. Her face was stern and her glare was menacing. She grabbed Ronnie's shoulder, which made him jump. Ricky looked at his mother and brother from the couch. As he expected the ass whooping to commence, he felt guilty for telling his mother, especially since his transgression with Sheelah was even worse.

"You're under punishment. You can't leave the house at all tomorrow," said Wilma.

"But why, mama?" asked Ronnie.

"For being too young and not using a god damn rubber."

Ronnie darted his vision at Ricky and then went to sit next to him on the couch, silently. At the time of the confrontation, Doreetha was standing at the edge of Wilma's bedroom, waiting for the right time to make her presence known.

"Hey, Wilma."

Wilma smiled at her good friend and put her arm on Doreetha's shoulder suddenly. Doreetha caught her footing and helped support Wilma.

"I just got off the phone with Lester and a few people dropped off some money earlier," said Doreetha.

Doreetha handed Wilma 50 dollars in cash along with a sheet of paper she pulled from her notebook.

"Thanks for doing this and watching the kids."

"Of course. See you tomorrow."

Doreetha waved at the boys and then exited the house. Wilma found her balance and made her way into the kitchen.

"Fat boy, you told!" whispered Ronnie as he pushed his

brother.

Ricky smirked and shrugged his shoulders. Ronnie decided not to escalate the conflict further. He lucked out by not getting beat and that was a victory for him. In the end, who could blame Ricky for his curiosity? Ricky too decided not to escalate the conflict. If he told Ronnie he got with Sheelah, he knew a beating would come his way and the blow would be devastating to a territorial Ronnie.

Sometimes the truth does not set you free, it imprisons you, thought Ricky.

Chapter 16: Fall 1966

A few months had passed and neither Sheelah nor Ricky revealed their dirty deed to Ronnie. Ronnie continued his relationship with her as if nothing had happened. Ricky's guilt had slowly dissipated as Ronnie's visits to the "shady shed" became more frequent. Everyone seemed to have his or her own routine. Ronnie would play the bongos and see Sheelah. Ricky would take care of Blackie and help his mother at the shop. Doreetha kept "half-assing" her babysitting job by taking the numbers. Wilma's routine was to have a drink before going into work, make sure she had enough to sip on for the day, then come home and have a drink before bed. Today, her routine was about to get disrupted.

Bailey's Salon was somewhat busy. Wilma curled Ruby's hair as Bryce styled the hair of Miss Moore. Miss Moore was a 65 year old Negro woman with gray hair. She was one of Bryce's loyal customers because she loved his quirky personality. Janette styled the hair of Miss Davis, a 58-year-old Negro woman. Janette was disguising all of her gray hair by dying it black.

"With all these afros and wigs, I wonder if anyone has style anymore?" mumbled Ruby.

In that moment Wilma was reminded of how her business was steadily declining since the Civil Rights legislation was passed. As much as she appreciated the government striving for equality, she did not appreciate the Negro client's reaction to it. Negroes felt the need to relocate to the suburbs with the white people and Afros became the new style to promote a level of independence. A million thoughts raced through Wilma's mind after hearing Ruby's comment, but she internalized them and continued curling.

"Wilma, you're pulling too hard," said Ruby.

Wilma's hand slipped and the curling iron seared Ruby's neck. She let out a high-pitched scream for the whole shop to hear. She stood up defiantly and ripped off her apron.

"Damn, Wilma!"

"I'm sorry," said Wilma halfheartedly.

"I smell alcohol on your breath!" yelled Ruby.

Wilma refused to make eye contact with Ruby. She kept

her head down and was ashamed. For the first time in her career as a cosmetologist, she burned a client with the iron.

"I'm never coming back to this shop."

Ruby stormed out and Wilma did not try to stop her. The shop was silent as Wilma picked up Ruby's apron. Bryce whispered to Miss Moore that he would be right back and then approached Wilma.

"Can I talk to you in the back?"

"Sure."

Wilma and Bryce entered the back room. It was full of clutter. Boxes on top of boxes were filled with new synthetic wigs. It was these wigs that also added to the decline of Bailey's Salon because the service of rolling, setting, and styling a wig was no longer needed. Wilma embraced the Roman's methodology and started selling the new product. Bryce shut the door behind him. He knew what he had to do even if it meant losing his job.

It was the right thing to do, he thought.

"This has gone way too far," said Bryce bluntly.

"I understand now why Kim liked it so much back here. It's...peaceful," said Wilma softly.

"Wilma, listen to me!"

Wilma shook her head to become more lucid. She looked Bryce in the eyes.

"I've seen you drink in here before and I've kept quiet because it never affected your work. But you just burned and lost a good customer," said Bryce forcefully yet sincerely.

"It was a simple mistake. Like you never make them," said Wilma defensively.

"This isn't about me, Wilma. I've talked to other customers. Martha, Louise, they all smell it on your breath."

"You know Kim has her own shop now?"

Bryce shook his head, not to become more lucid, but out of annoyance for Wilma changing the subject.

"She quit because of you."

"Well, forget that. Wilma, you still owe me money for the supply delivery I paid for. I'm taking it from the register."

Wilma did not think she owed Bryce anything. He walked

out of the backroom with Wilma following. Bryce attempted to open the register. Wilma grabbed Bryce's shoulders and tried to pull him away from the register. She fell to the floor, embarrassingly.

"Wilma!" yelled Janette.

Janette ran to Wilma and helped her up. Wilma was livid.

"You're fired! Get out of my shop, you...you..Fag!"

Bryce, along with everyone else, stared at Wilma in disbelief. Never before had Wilma used such crude language, at least in a professional setting. Wilma hated the word "fag." She always considered herself to have an open and understanding mind when it came to homosexuals, but after what happened with Fritz, her mind became closed off and bitter. Bryce reached his hand into the now open register and took a handful of bills. He stuffed it into his pocket and then calmly walked to his station. Wilma was shaking as she watched Bryce like a hawk. Bryce put his supplies in his bag and walked to the exit. He turned back toward Wilma before leaving.

"Your salon's dead anyway, bitch."

Bryce slammed the door behind him. The entrance bell fell off the door. The most boisterous, annoying, and nosy worker was gone. At first Wilma mentally rejoiced until she remembered people like Miss Moore and all the other people who came to her shop only for Bryce. As much as she did not like Bryce, he brought in business. Wilma let her emotions get the best of her but no one was about to disrespect her like that. No one.

"Janette, when you're done with Miss Davis you can go home. I'm closing early today."

Janette nodded slowly, processing what had just happened. Wilma approached a dumbfounded Miss Moore and continued styling where Bryce had left off. No one spoke the rest of the day, fearful of a possible altercation with Wilma.

Back at the house, Doreetha wrote diligently in her black notepad while cradling the rotary phone in her shoulder. She was recording a long list of three number combinations. In the last three years, her speed had gotten faster and she was more organized. She definitely enjoyed her administrative job more than her job in the street. She was happy to use her brain to accumulate wealth as opposed to her body.

"And how much did you want on that?" asked Doreetha into the phone.

Doreetha scribbled "$2.00" next to the numbers "619."

"All right. You're all set."

Doreetha hung up the phone and proceeded to the kitchen. She saw Ricky frying chicken on the cast iron skillet. The smell was intoxicating and caused Doreetha to wet her lips. She was impressed to see that Ricky set the table and was awaiting his mother's arrival.

"Why are so many people calling?" asked Ricky curiously.

Doreetha figured that Wilma would not want her ten-year-old son understanding the intricacies of such an illegal process.

"Everybody loves your mother," replied Doreetha.

"What do you write in that notebook?" asked Ricky as he flipped a chicken breast.

"The messages they want to leave."

Ronnie had ceased playing his bongos and overheard the

conversation from the living room. He decided to "cut the bullshit" and educate his younger brother.

"Shut up, you know she's taking the numbers for Mama now," yelled Ronnie from the other room.

The phone rang loudly from Wilma's bedroom, which caused Doreetha to rush out and get it. Ricky and Ronnie made eye contact as Ricky transferred cornbread from the oven to a plate on the table.

"How is banging those bongos any fun?" asked Ricky.

"How is cooking fun?" retorted Ronnie snidely.

Ricky gave a disgruntled look and almost considered tampering with his chicken, but a good chef would never stoop to such lows.

In Wilma's bedroom, Doreetha checked her watch before picking up the phone. She knew who it was.

"Wilma?"

It was Wilma. And so began a five-minute exchange in which Doreetha carefully read Wilma all of her recordings for the day. Wilma made her own list and thanked Doreetha for her

"What's John L. talking about Big Nick hit for 10 grand. You didn't give me no number for Nick."

A few seconds passed before Doreetha responded. Wilma could hear Doreetha take in a deep breath over the phone. Wilma was not looking forward to this response.

"Oh, Wilma. He did call...I forgot to write it down. I'm so sorry."

Wilma took a few seconds of her own to process this situation before giving her response. Siphoning specificity was first on the list.

"What did he play?" asked Wilma.

"I think it was 5-1-6 or something like that."

Wilma's mouth dropped as she looked at what Mr. Reeve had played on the sheet of paper. Mr. Reeve's bet was small but Big Nick lived up to his name and went big. She slammed down the phone receiver and put her head in her hands. A loud knocking pierced the scene and caused Wilma to jump. She yelled at the unwelcomed guest from the counter.

"We're closed!"

Wilma knew the acoustics of her shop well enough to know that the person outside heard her, yet the knocking persisted. Wilma walked to the door and peeked through the front window. The burly black man that was Big Nick stood outside her shop with a recently extinguished cigar at his feet. Wilma had met Big Nick once before. John L. had brought her to The 20 Grand with Doreetha last summer. He was very charming but like any gangster, there was a mean streak to him. There was a moment in the club in which Big Nick caught Wilma staring at him. Before he winked at her like most men did, she noticed a certain level of deadness in his eyes. He appeared to be a man whose spirit was broken. It made Wilma curious about his past but she would never dare to ask. At this present moment, Wilma wanted nothing more than to ignore him but that would only be delaying the inevitable. Wilma opened the door.

"Hi, Nick."

"Hi, Wilma. I don't mean to be a burden but you know I hit for 10 grand tonight."

Wilma opened the door all the way so Big Nick could

waddle on in.

"Yeah. I just found out. It's gonna take me a few days."

"Can you please give me some of it now? I'm flat broke."

Big Nick's wardrobe said otherwise. Wilma's initial instinct was to hold her ground and not give him any money but then that little inhibitor called fear kicked in.

"Wait here," said Wilma.

Wilma walked to the backroom, slowly. During the whole trek she was having a mental tug of war over if she had made the right decision. Once she opened the safe she knew the decision had been made. Wilma pulled out a large stack of cash. She counted the money and stuffed it into a small brown bag.

In Wilma's absence, Big Nick walked around the salon and took it in. He picked up a pair of scissors from one of the stations. He used the ends of the scissors to clean the dirt out from under his fingernails. Wilma exited the backroom and approached him.

"Here's six grand. I can get you the rest by Monday," said Wilma flatly.

Big Nick continued cleaning his nails with the shears and mindlessly stared at Wilma. She once again noticed the listlessness behind his big brown eyes. Big Nick put the scissors down on the counter in front of Wilma. He grabbed the bag from Wilma's hand and stuffed it into his coat. He smiled at Wilma before kissing her on the cheek. Wilma cringed.

"Thank you so much, Wilma."

Wilma nodded hesitantly. She quickly moved to the front door and opened it up. A cold breeze chilled Wilma to the bone as Big Nick left. After the door shut, Wilma wound up her leg and kicked a trash can as hard as she could. It flew across the shop and debris went everywhere.

"Those mother fuckers," she mumbled under her breath.

Wilma was played in a game that she just lost control of.

Ricky and Ronnie spent their evening soaking up one of pop culture's most influential hero of the time; *Batman*. During the battle scenes, the boys would hit each other and make the show's sound effects.

"BAM! POW! WHAM!"

The show framed violence in a more entertaining way compared to all of the stuff the boys had seen in Detroit and on the news. John L. had stormed in while the show was on and went right to Wilma's bedroom where Doreetha was. Before Ricky and Ronnie could even process John L.'s arrival, Doreetha screamed in agony in between, what sounded like, slaps. John L. proceeded to drag her out of the house, not saying anything to the boys before they left. It was Ricky's initial instinct to call Mama but Ronnie assured him that she already left the shop.

Fifteen minutes later, Wilma arrived. Ricky stood up quickly and ran to his mother while Ronnie stayed seated, more interested in Batman fighting crime.

"Mama, John L. came and he beat Doreetha!" said Ricky.

Wilma was not fazed by Ricky's comment, especially after she had just talked to John L. about what happened. She went to her bedroom and took note of the messiness that most likely resulted from their scuffle.

"Where are they now?" asked Wilma calmly.

"John L. dragged her out of the house. We can't find

Blackie either," said Ricky.

"I gotta eat something," said Wilma.

Wilma sat down on the couch next to Ronnie. Both sons gauged how drained she was. Ricky immediately rushed to the kitchen and brought a plate of food to Wilma, like the devoted son he was. Wilma smiled as she took the plate. From all the craziness and deception that clouded her day, Ricky represented a glimmer of hope. No matter what scheme Doreetha and Big Nick had concocted, Wilma still had her boys. She still had her family. Although this scam would be a big financial blow to her business, she took this time to appreciate her sons and the fact that she had a roof over her head. However, these thoughts were fleeting as nervousness and fear overtook her. These were emotions that led her to wash down her chicken with Seagram's gin.

John L. drove his Cadillac, cracking the biggest smile on his face. Doreetha sat in the front seat with a face that was a mirror opposite of John L.'s.

"You think they believed it?" asked Doreetha nervously.

"The way you screamed? What a performance."

Doreetha put her head down, feeling solemn about how Wilma was affected. Over the years, they cultivated a friendship and a level of trust, which now meant nothing. Besides her colleagues on the street, Wilma was the closest thing Doreetha had to a true friend. During that car ride all she could do was convince herself that her loyalty was still to John L. and the money they made. John L. parked his car outside The 20 Grand. The lights from the club illuminated the lot and served as a beacon for the patrons entering.

"Wait here," said John L. flatly.

Doreetha needed to turn off the guilty thoughts in her head, which led her to turn on the radio. "Stop in the Name of Love" by The Supremes played as Doreetha bobbed her head.

John L. walked into the club expeditiously and surveyed it for Big Nick. He spotted the "Neanderthal" throwing dollar bills onto a table for a round of drinks. Three sexy women in skimpy clothes sat around and ogled him and his money, but mostly his money.

"Looks like you got it."

Big Nick ignored John L. and instead chose to make out with one of the girls. John L.'s patience was wearing thin. He waited three years to make this move with Big Nick and now he was so close to getting the money he thought he deserved. He could not wait any longer.

"I'd like it if we did this now," said John L. firmly.

Big Nick stopped kissing and turned to John L.

"Grab a girl, get a drink. We're celebrating tonight!"

"Now," said John L. bluntly.

"All right. Calm the fuck down."

Big Nick sat up, much to the dismay of the whores around him. He followed John L. out the side door.

John L. already knew which car was Big Nick's and arrived at it before he could. He was parked close enough to the alley that no one from the entrance could see them. However, from John L.'s car, Doreetha could see them through the rear view mirror, yet she was far enough away for neither of them to see her.

"You think we got away with it?" asked Big Nick.

"Yeah. If Wilma knew and she told Silverman, you'd already be dead."

"She still has to pay me the rest on Monday," said Big Nick.

"How much she have?"

"Your cuts in the trunk."

Big Nick popped open the trunk and nodded his head to a brown paper bag sitting on top of a bunch of clear garbage bags. John L. reached for the bag and picked it up, only to realize that it was empty. Just as John L. turned around, Big Nick took out his Saturday night special and shot him in the forehead.

Doreetha screamed as The Supremes chorus blasted in the car. She covered her mouth and crouched down in the seat. She kept her mouth covered to keep the sound of her hyperventilating to a dull roar.

Big Nick grabbed the fallen body and quickly stuffed it in the trunk. He closed the trunk and looked around to make sure no one saw him. He didn't want to have to kill two people in one night. The disposal was always such a messy chore for him.

Doreetha peeked out the window to see Big Nick driving away. She was spared...for now. She exited the car slowly and her walk turned into a sprint. She needed to get out of town. She needed to change her life.

The next morning, Wilma felt like everything was in slow motion. She was only mildly drunk but the weight of losing that money was heavy. Also, the thought of Silverman knowing would be detrimental to her business and maybe even her life.

I can't tell Silverman. He would kill me, thought Wilma.

At the shop, Wilma stood at the counter and wrote on a clipboard. She made a master list of all of the supplies in her shop. It was mindless work that gave her time to reflect on the scam and what she would do next. There was a sudden knock on the front door, which caused Wilma to jump. Wilma looked out the window and saw Shirley. A relieved Wilma let her in.

"I know you're not open yet, but I want to talk," said Shirley.

"I gotta do inventory but I'm listening."

Wilma studied her clipboard and walked away from

Shirley to one of the stations.

"Been awhile, stranger. Haven't seen you at Chubby's lately."

"Drinks are too expensive," said Wilma nonchalantly.

Wilma navigated to each station, organizing and counting the hair supplies. Shirley was concerned about Wilma's distance and decided to grab her arm. They made eye contact.

"Wilma, I know I haven't seen you much but please tell me what's going on?"

Wilma took in the sincerity in Shirley's voice. She recalled on all of the fond memories they had and how she had been a loyal friend throughout the years. Although Wilma swore she would not tell anyone about last night's extortion, she needed to vent. Shirley was the only person in her life right now who could understand.

"Doreetha said she forgot to write down Big Nick's number. He won a lot...I lost a lot."

"Did you tell Silverman?" asked Shirley swiftly.

"No. I paid him myself. With my share."

"Are you crazy? You gotta tell Silverman, Wilma."

"No," said Wilma assertively.

"He can help you out."

"This one I gotta handle myself."

"Wilma..."

"Please, Shirley. On our friendship, please don't tell him."

Wilma did not expect Shirley to suggest telling Mr. Silverman. She only hoped that her friendship meant enough to Shirley as it did to her so Shirley would not cross that line.

Later that night it rained heavily in the city of Detroit. The windshield wipers of Shirley's red Cadillac moved back and forth rapidly, only to yield minimal visibility. Shirley arrived at her destination with bated breath. She exited the car in her matching raincoat and ran to the entrance door of Silverman's Cleaners. She was able to stay dry under the awning as she looked through the window passed the "We're Closed" sign. All she could see was an endless line of washers and dryers, in dim lighting, with not a soul in sight. That was until Moe came out from the side office. He glanced at Shirley and let her in.

"Hey, Moe. How are you, sweetie?"

Without saying a word, Moe turned and walked back toward the office. Shirley followed behind, shrugging off his rudeness. Shirley entered the office and saw Mr. Silverman behind his desk, smoking a cigarette. The room was so smoky that it instantly reminded her of her visibility issues in the car. Shirley sat in a seat across from the desk.

"Thanks, Moe," said Mr. Silverman.

Moe gave a decisive nod and exited the office, shutting the door behind him.

"What's going on, Shirley?"

"This 'Big Nick' has been spending your money all over town. Well...Wilma's money."

"He's back to armed robbery again?"

"He hit her for ten grand. Doreetha didn't write it down."

For a second, Shirley felt the weight of guilt come over her. It was like a heavy pressure on her chest. She had lied to Wilma about not telling Mr. Silverman, but in her heart she knew it was the right thing to do. She trusted the man enough to clean up the mess. Mr. Silverman's specialty was cleaning, after all.

"Sounds like a scam to me," said Mr. Silverman.

"I think so..."

"Keep an eye on Wilma. Soldiers are coming home and bringing business opportunities with them. I need you and Jerry on the street."

Shirley did not give herself enough time to process that statement before blurting out her original question she intended to ask, out of her friendship with Wilma.

"Can you give her some money back? She's struggling."

As much as Mr. Silverman did not want a drug market in his city, he had his orders. He begrudgingly retorted with a statement, he felt, better highlighted the impending fiasco as financially viable as opposed to any other grave consequence.

"Get her on board with this new venture and she won't miss ten thousand dollars."

Both Shirley and Mr. Silverman left that office unsatisfied that night, only to enter an even more dreary atmosphere that embodied the transition of Autumn to Winter in Michigan.

Chapter 17: Christmas 1966

Even on Christmas Eve, The 20 Grand was packed. It was filled with people who were not necessarily the most religious and treated the holiday as an even bigger excuse to party. Big Nick was one of those people. And now that he was more well off after the scam, he found himself spending more money on the sultry sinning of drinking and receiving dances from the type of girls he could never get to work for him in the street, but were the finest in the city. He did, however, attract a new girl that night. A girl who flaunted her voluptuous body by indicating she was looking for "a Daddy." They both festively dressed for the occasion. Big Nick wore a bright red suit and the girl wore a green dress. As Big Nick and "his new girl" exited the club, he knew he was going to have a merry Christmas.

A 1966 black Buick Electra 225 pulled up to the curb. The passenger window rolled down and a cigarette butt was flicked near Big Nick's feet. Big Nick gazed into the open window finding a white man, he thought looked familiar, but could not place where he knew him from. The driver, Moe, knew who he was and had found the guy he was looking for.

"Excuse me," said Moe.

Big Nick locked eyes with Moe as "his new girl" dazed off into space, clearly on something.

"Are you Nicholas Nitty?" asked Moe firmly.

"Who's asking?"

"A potential employer."

Big Nick and John L. may not have seen eye to eye on everything, especially when it came to money, but if there was one thing they agreed on, it was this hesitance to work with white people. This stemmed mostly out of anger and hatred for the abuse of white supremacy over the decades, but also out of genuine fear of that power.

"Not interested," said Big Nick flatly.

Moe got out of the car suddenly and walked toward Big Nick. At first, it was hard seeing where the car ended and his body began for he wore a black trench coat that matched the paint of his car.

"Back the fuck up," said Big Nick.

Big Nick pulled out a black pistol from his front pocket and held it to his side. Moe stopped in his tracks and put his hands up. This wasn't the first time someone pulled a gun on Moe and he would be damned if it was his last.

"We have a lot of respect for you, Nick. We've been looking at you for some time."

"Who the fuck are you?"

"Someone like you. Someone who is trying to make as much money as he can before his last heartbeat."

Big Nick stared at Moe, skeptically. Between the car, the smooth talking, and the bravery he had shown, Big Nick decided then in there that Moe was mob. Big Nick thought that he could put his hatred of white folk aside as long as business was fruitful. He still held the gun at his side as he sized up Moe further.

"Someone who was asked by Mr. Silverman to set up a meeting with you. Tonight."

In that moment, the metaphorical light bulb in Big Nick's head illuminated. Anyone who was anyone knew who Mr. Silverman was. His name was synonymous with Detroit's Jewish

Mob presence, a true descendent of the Purple Gang.

"On Christmas Eve?" asked Big Nick incredulously.

Moe laughed and put his hands down.

"We're Jewish."

Big Nick smirked and put away his gun. He turned to "his new girl" who was standing there chain-smoking due to nervousness from the troublesome situation.

"I'll meet you back here tomorrow night."

Big Nick gave her a long kiss goodnight. As she walked down the alley, her high heels made a loud clacking noise. Big Nick could not help but stare at her rear end before Moe snapped him out of it.

"Hop in."

Moe got in the driver seat and Big Nick entered the passenger seat. Moe sped down the street, which had reminded him of his times driving with John L. For a split second, Big Nick regretted killing John L. He was his only friend after all. But that sentiment quickly dissipated and was replaced by a new one.

Friendships fade, relationships die, money is forever.

Big Nick sat silently in the passenger seat as Moe drove through Detroit. All Big Nick could think about was the notoriety and respect he would finally get if he became a "made man." Big Nick also wondered where Moe was taking him, but he was able to make out Checker's Barbeque through the snow covered window. A green Chrysler Imperial stood out amongst the cars parallel parked on the street. Moe pulled the car into an alley next to the restaurant.

"Are you hungry?" asked Moe.

Big Nick could always go for Checker's famous barbecue ribs but then recalled how messy they were and how sauce splattering all over his suit may not make him out to be the most desirable candidate for the job.

"No," retorted Big Nick.

"Wait here."

Moe exited the car and walked down the alley. Big Nick watched as Moe turned the corner toward Checker's. As much as Big Nick wanted to believe this was a genuine opportunity, he graduated from John L.'s school of thought with regards to not trusting "the white man." Big Nick took out his pistol and made sure it was loaded and it was.

Mr. Silverman sat at a table and cut the final piece of barbecue duck. He chewed and swallowed with satisfaction. Moe then entered which satisfied Mr. Silverman even more. The two well-dressed men made eye contact for a second, but no words were exchanged. Moe approached the counter to order food. Mr. Silverman got up, threw his wrappers in the garbage can, and put on his overcoat before exiting the restaurant.

Mr. Silverman strolled down the alley toward Moe's car. Big Nick watched Mr. Silverman intently. Big Nick expected Mr. Silverman to be taller and more menacing.

He's just some old white guy, he thought.

Mr. Silverman opened the car door and sat in the driver seat.

"Mr. Nitty."

Mr. Silverman extended his hand for a shake and Big Nick followed suit. Big Nick was taken aback by how cold Mr. Silverman's hand was.

"Never thought I'd meet the notorious Mr. Silverman."

"Life is full of surprises."

Mr. Silverman lit a cigarette and blew the smoke in Big Nick's face. A seasoned smoker such as Big Nick usually did not mind the smoke, but intentionally blowing it in his face did bother him. It just did not bother him enough to say something.

"I need a driver. Twice a week. Going to Cincinnati and Buffalo. These are very important shipments."

"A driver? Here I thought I was getting my hands dirty."

"There will be advancement opportunities."

As good as the offer sounded, Big Nick's was skeptical.

"Why me? Why now?" asked Big Nick.

"I like your style, Nicholas. You're not afraid to take what you want.

"That's the attitude we need. But I do have one question."

Big Nick raised his eyebrows curiously.

"Are you a junkie?"

Big Nick had his drug binges in the past but those days were over. The only thing he was addicted to now was money.

"No."

"Cause you can't be fucking up our supply," said Mr. Silverman firmly.

"No. I smoke a little weed and drink. That's it."

"Meet me at Silverman's Cleaners Monday morning."

Mr. Silverman turned to exit the vehicle but Big Nick was not sold. He interjected.

"Wait. How much it pay?"

"We'll talk Monday."

Mr. Silverman reached into his coat pocket. Big Nick jumped at this and almost reached for his gun.

"Take this as a token of my good will."

Mr. Silverman pulled out a large cigar and handed it to Big Nick. Big Nick grabbed it, smiled, and smelled it. It had the aroma of the freshest tobacco he had ever smelled.

"Everyone should smoke a Cohiba before they die."

Mr. Silverman lit Big Nick's cigar with his lighter before exiting the vehicle. Mr. Silverman left the door ajar.

"Hey! Shut the door!" yelled Big Nick.

Mr. Silverman either did not hear him or ignored him as he walked up the alley, back toward Checker's. Big Nick leaned in to close the driver door as he took a long drag from his cigar. In that moment, the passenger door swung open swiftly. Moe shot Big Nick in the head and blood splattered onto the windshield. Moe then walked to the driver's side, started the engine, and drove off to dispose of the body and the car. In his green Imperial, Mr. Silverman watched Moe drive away with Big Nick's corpse and was content that Wilma was avenged and justice was served.

Chapter 18: Summer 1967

It wasn't the sizzling heat that drove American citizens off the edge during the summer of 1967. It wasn't the scorching sun that caused a Tampa police officer to shoot an alleged Negro shoplifter, spawning several days of rioting in the streets. It wasn't the east coast humidity that yielded that same kind of chaos in Newark and Buffalo that summer. The real fuel to this fire was the racial tension still present in a nation that, even the recent Civil Rights legislation, could not extinguish. Wilma and many other citizens had thought that this "wildfire" would not spread to a more liberal city such as Detroit. They were gravely mistaken.

For years, Detroit officers turned the other way when it came to the mass illegality of 12th Street. All the cops that frequented there were dirty, but at 3:30 in the morning of July 23, a pair of "squeaky-clean" officers infiltrated one of the speakeasies. The Negro officers wore plain clothes to blend in and take in the party. It was hard for them to maneuver through what seemed to be close to a hundred people crowding around, drinking and gambling.

A typical "12th Street party" during that time usually catered to between 30 and 40 patrons, but this was a special event. Although it was a celebration for two returning Vietnam veterans, that commemoration of patriotism did not stop the disguised officers from exacting their extreme view of "law and order." After a signal was given, a swarm of police officers busted through the doors of the Blind Pig wielding shotguns, handguns, and billy clubs. Pandemonium erupted as guilty men and women ran out of the club in droves while Detroit officers arrested and detained as many as they could get their hands on. Guests poured out of the establishment as if they were avoiding the plague.

Officers began leading people upstairs to hold them until more paddy wagons arrived. The officers of the 10th Precinct, in which 12th Street was located, only had access to one paddy wagon, which could fit between roughly twelve to fourteen prisoners. From the phone inside the Blind Pig, an officer made calls to the 6th, 11th, and 13th precincts to request more paddy wagons for transporting all of the "criminals." It was a very tense hour before the cavalry would arrive. One officer peered out the window down on 12th Street. What had originally been 30 bystanders roaming the street, turned into over 200 people standing and yelling outside the Blind Pig.

One of the pedestrians, despite the warm weather, wore a long sleeved green shirt. He would later be dubbed as "Green Sleeves" by the Detroit Police Department. Green Sleeves stood on top of a car as the new paddy wagons pulled up. Enraged at what he viewed as; racial profiling, he would not stand for the raid to go on any longer. He yelled boisterously for the whole neighborhood to hear.

"We can't let them take our people away! This is our street! Let's get them whiteys!"

The mostly Negro crowd was getting riled up as the police officers became more nervous. The officers began the transfer of the detained partygoers into the paddy wagons. Green Sleeves escalated the situation by throwing a brick at the back window of one of the police cruisers. Soon everyone was throwing bricks and bottles. The paddy wagons were able to leave the area safely, but the city would not be safe. Incensed by the "racial injustice" at the Blind Pig, the crowd of 200 blossomed to 10,000 by noon, burning and looting their way down 12th Street.

Mayor Cavanagh instructed the police officers not to shoot any looters so there would be no provocation. Cavanagh, like many others, hoped that the crowd would disperse on its own without anyone getting hurt. These hopes were lofty after three days of continual rioting caused Governor George Romney to deploy the National Guard. The Guard would not adhere to the "no shooting policy" of the Detroit Police Department, resulting in more deaths than there needed to be. Despite praising peaceful solutions to the riots in public, in a private moment, much like his son's eventual "47% comment," Governor Romney had blurted out:

"If anyone is seen looting, shoot to kill."

There were people within the crowd that did desire a nonviolent resolution for the madness. Detroit Tigers Left-

Fielder, Willie Horton, hoped that his reputation and popularity would get the rioters to listen. In his Tiger's uniform, he stood on top of a car and urged people to stop looting and pillaging.

"Go home! Please! Stop this!" pleaded Horton.

Most of the looters and rioters ignored the star player but one comment from an angered Negro stood out.

"What do you care, Horton? You got your money."

Willie Horton was not the selfish person this man made him out to be. He genuinely cared about his community and wanted dearly to disperse the violence. It would be a futile effort.

Nearby, Negro Representative of Michigan's 1st District, John Conyers, also stood on a car to try and calm the mob. Even yelling into a bullhorn did not change anything.

"Stop this madness! Go to your homes!"

His pleas were met with confrontation as people threw rocks and yelled at him.

"Get out of here you Uncle Tom, mother fucker!" one rioter yelled.

Despite the good intentions of these affluent men, the

rioting would rage on.

Detroit had turned into a war zone. Electricity was cut off and fire spread from 12th Street businesses to Linwood. Chubby's After Hour Joint, Hardy's Drug Store, The Linoleum Paint Company, and Famous Furniture were a few of the many businesses that burned to the ground. As "Hell on Earth" was attempted to be put out by the fire department, officers were stationed to protect the J.L Hudson building, Detroit's biggest piece of architecture. Tanks were now commonplace and they were not just for show. A man that had lit a cigarette in his apartment complex, which to a "trigger happy" National guardsman, was perceived as a spark of gunfire. The building was pummeled by an endless array of bullets from a .50 caliber machine gun on the tank. Four-year-old Tanya Blanding was added to the list of casualties.

Cavanagh and Romney sought another solution to bring stability to the situation. They took their concerns to President Johnson and asked for federal troops to assist the officers and guardsmen. Johnson, a democrat, saw this fiasco as an opportunity to discredit Romney, a republican contender for the 1968 election. Johnson played politics by not only wasting time bringing in the troops, but painted Governor Romney as incompetent during a national address, stating that;

"Romney and the local officials were unable to bring the situation under control."

Although it was a move to garner political points by smearing Romney, Johnson was right. It took the arrival of the army troops to really begin disbanding the looters. But it was not always done civilly. Since the electricity was cut off in the residences, perishable food from refrigerators was no longer edible for the hungry citizens. A group of teenagers broke into an A&P Supermarket to get as much food as they could. Two National Guardsmen exited a green jeep parked in front of the supermarket. The "looters" were shot dead through the supermarket window. The atrocious killings of mostly Negro citizens enraged the Black Panthers organization, who decided to take matters into their own hands. They began perching on top of rooftops and shot at officers, guardsmen, and army men in order to protect the endangered black folk.

From July 23rd to July 28th, Detroit burned and Wilma Bailey watched the whole thing unfold on television. She closed her shop when the violence started and could only pray that there would be no damage. Ricky and Ronnie were quarantined to the living room, close to Wilma. Wilma made that decision when she saw a tank pull up in the schoolyard. Ricky and Ronnie would return to school when education became more of a priority than protection.

Ricky obeyed his mother by staying in the living room, but his mind wandered outside the home. The large tank stationed at Brady Elementary across the street, fascinated him. It was a massive piece of machinery that wielded so much power. Ricky thought of getting inside it to try and scare all the bullies that made fun of his weight. Ronnie was transfixed by the action on TV and his nose almost touched the screen. He admired The Black Panthers who were seen sniping officers from the rooftops. Although Ronnie was not partial to violence, he definitely enjoyed watching it. The volume on the television was lower, for

Wilma instead chose to listen to Aretha Franklin's "Mary Don't You Weep" on her record player. She sat on the couch and sipped on a glass of Seagram's gin as she drifted in and out of consciousness.

"Mama!" shrieked Ronnie.

Wilma jolted awake, almost spilling her drink on herself. Ronnie pointed at the television set as Wilma stood up. Wilma dropped her glass onto the carpeted floor, liquid pouring out of the glass and streaming in between her bare toes. She was stunned silent when she processed what she saw on the screen. It was her salon burning up in flames. Her successful business, her place of refuge, her second home was now a memory.

"I'm sorry, Mama," said Ronnie softly.

Ricky ran from the window and hugged Wilma, who, after a few seconds of stillness, hugged back. The phone rang and pierced the silence. Wilma picked it up slowly.

"Hello."

"Watching the news?" asked Jack.

Jack sat on his own respective couch in his house on

Murray Hill, a more affluent neighborhood than Wilma's. Like his ex-wife, and sons, he watched the news in awe and wanted to make sure Wilma was aware of her shop's destruction.

"Yeah. I am," said Wilma.

"What are you going to do now?"

Wilma could not think. She could barely even breathe. The last person she wanted to talk to in that moment was a man who betrayed her. A man who was probably calling just to rub her face in why the business was a bad idea in the first place. Wilma snapped.

"Just make sure you send the child support check next week."

Wilma hung up the phone, abruptly. All she wanted to do was scream, but she did not want to show weakness in front of her sons. She needed to be strong for them. She grabbed a rag from the kitchen and soaked up the spilt gin on the carpet and tried to avoid shedding tears as she dried up the liquid.

"Turn off the television, Ronnie."

This was the one time Ronnie did not put up a fuss about

turning off the television.

What started out as a party for Vietnam Veterans, turned into one of the worst riots in American history. 43 people died with 33 of them being Negroes. 473 were injured, and 7,231 people were arrested. Bailey's Salon had been one of the 2,509 stores looted or burned. Mayor Cavanagh summed up the sentiment of the citizens as he looked out on the damage:

"Today we stand amidst the ashes of our hopes. We hoped against hope that what we had been doing was enough to prevent a riot. It was not enough."

The city had lost its hope but one voice strived to get it back. Inside the WJLB Radio Station, Martha Jean "The Queen," one of Detroit's most popular radio personalities, sat in front of a large microphone and addressed a broken city. "Without a Song" by James Cleveland played aptly in the background as she spoke.

"Good Afternoon, Detroit. It's Martha Jean "The Queen" on WJLB. It's the top of the hour and we got a great line up for you today. But I want to take this time to talk about our city. Our home. We had a hard summer, Detroit. Now I know our political leaders are saying it was a race riot, but we know better, Detroit. This wasn't about race. White folks, we need you like you need us. This is our city. Now it's time to clean up our neighborhoods and rebuild. Together."

The song faded out as she stopped "preaching." Her tone then went from somber to zany.

"Well, it's time to pay the bills. I want you to check out Al's Fried Chicken. Go get that pint of fries for 35 cents. And all the hot sauce and ketchup you can eat! Tell 'em *The Queen* sent you."

"The Queen" managed to put smiles on the faces of the majority of listeners that day. But a lot more inspiration would have to be invoked in order to shift the pessimistic perspectives of Detroit's citizens. The Civil Rights legislation had knocked down the barriers in the housing market, which prompted a mass exodus of black and white citizens alike, but the riots increased that rate, exponentially. This left the city's next generation with no positive role models to look up to. The heroin addicts coming back from Vietnam, the dealers that supplied them, and the mob that promoted the drugs in the communities of color, would run rampant. Detroit's dark transformation had begun: economically with the massive drug use in the squandering auto industry and emotionally by the break up of families and the destruction of relationships. There was no going back.

Chapter 19: Fall 1967-Summer 1968

Wilma sat at the kitchen table peeling potatoes in between taking sips from her glass filled with a clear liquid and three ice cubes. The entire kitchen counter was covered with ingredients to make a great Thanksgiving feast. All she needed to get was the turkey. A few months had passed since her beloved shop burned and Wilma found refuge in cooking. It was a therapeutic process that kept her mind off of everything that she lost, She shifted her focus onto what she was thankful for; that she could still put food on the table. Wilma dropped her peeler suddenly when she gazed upon a large Canadian goose strut its way into the kitchen. The goose tilted its head at Wilma, almost as if she was the one that did not belong in this environment.

"Ronnie! Ricky! Get in here!"

Ronnie and Ricky rushed into the kitchen from the living room, both clearly disappointed by their mother's discovery of their feathered friend.

"There you are, Goose," said Ronnie.

"You named the goose, Goose?" chimed in Ricky.

"What's a good name then, Ricky? Spike?"

"Why the hell is there a bird in my house?" said Wilma anxiously.

Ricky looked at Ronnie, expecting his older brother to answer so he wouldn't be caught lying. Ricky was bad at lying, especially to his mother who could read him like a book.

"He walked in," said Ronnie confidently.

Wilma darted her gaze at Ricky.

"Where did this goose come from, Ricky?"

Ricky looked at Ronnie and then at his mother. Wilma's menacing stare made Ricky too nervous to lie, as much as he wanted to be cool in front of Ronnie.

"Brady," said Ricky softly.

"What? The school is closed," said Wilma.

"Ronnie took him when the petting zoo came."

"Thanks a lot, fat boy," said Ronnie.

"We can't have a goose living here, boys."

"What about the alligators?"

Ricky was on a roll with telling the truth, which prompted

Ronnie to push his younger brother.

"Wow. Really Ricky?"

"Do not tell me there are alligators in this house," expelled Wilma.

Ricky and Ronnie stared at the ground, silently. Ronnie pet a stoic Goose.

"Where are they?" inquired Wilma loudly.

Ricky led the way to Ronnie's bedroom. He pulled off the blanket to expose two baby alligators planted on the bed. Wilma could not believe it.

"Not in my house."

Wilma grabbed both gators by their tails and exited the room. She entered the bathroom and with no hesitance at all, tossed the gators into the toilet. She flushed them as Ricky and Ronnie watched from hallway. Ricky turned to face his brother.

"I'm sorry," said Ricky.

"I don't care. As long as she don't mess with Goose."

Wilma left the bathroom and confronted her oldest son.

"Ronnie, I don't want you bringing anymore animals into

this house."

"Can I at least keep Goose, Mama?"

"Just for tonight."

"Can we go to the parade now?" asked Ricky.

"Just be back by 6 for dinner."

Ronnie approached Goose in the kitchen and ran behind him to force him into Ronnie's bedroom. Next to his bed was a large cardboard box, which served as a dwelling for Goose. Ronnie made sure Goose was inside before leaving with Ricky for the Thanksgiving Day parade.

As the clock struck six, Wilma was finally done cooking the largest meal she had made in a long time. She had considered inviting relatives over, but her alcoholism had seriously isolated herself from her family. She could also do without the silent and verbal judgments from her family members with regards to how much she drank. All that mattered to her was that herself and her boys were taken care of this holiday season. No one else mattered. She set the table with an array of different foods. A bowl of sweet potatoes, macaroni and cheese, cornbread, and a large roasting pan filled the table. Ricky and Ronnie's timing was impeccable as they arrived just as Wilma put the last of the utensils on the table.

"How was the parade?" asked Wilma.

"It was okay. Bozo was there," said Ricky.

"Scary ass clown," muttered Ronnie.

Ronnie proceeded to his bedroom to check on Goose. Ricky sat down at the table and started eating before anyone else. He took a large portion of the meat and stuffed his face.

"This is delicious, Mama," said Ricky.

"I'm glad you like it," said Wilma.

Ronnie scoured his bedroom, searching for his latest pet.

"Mama, where's Goose?" yelled Ronnie from his room.

Wilma had just finished making up her plate, and like Ricky, cherished the taste of the main course before diving into the side dishes.

For Michiganders, spring was a coveted season. Its arrival meant that the long and dreary winter that had plagued the state for, what felt like half a year, was now a distant memory. Flowers were now blooming. The sun was now shining. But the thawing of the state was not always enough to liven up spirits, especially in the midst of tragedy.

Detroiters of all ages and creeds were marching in the streets on the early morning of April 5, 1968. Ronnie and a slew of his classmates ditched school and joined the crowd. Ronnie knew the significance of this demonstration and he also knew how much Ricky would want to be apart of it. The hundreds of marchers were now making their way towards Brady Elementary. Ronnie ran across the schoolyard, where a tank once sat menacingly a year before, and set his sights on a first floor window of the school. Ronnie knew that Ricky's homeroom was Miss Clay and remembered which window was hers from his previous education at Brady. Ronnie and 15 to 20 classmates ran up to the window because what had happened the night before created an overwhelming feeling of urgency in them, and people across the nation. Ronnie opened the window from the outside. Ricky could not believe his eyes when he saw Ronnie and the crowd outside the window.

"Ricky, let's go!" yelled Ronnie into the classroom.

The attention of everyone in the room was now Ronnie's, including the teacher's.

"Get away from that window!" yelled Miss Clay.

As she made her way to the window, the students murmured and watched an unfazed Ronnie remain there with his classmates. Ronnie was staring at his younger brother during the few seconds it took for Miss Clay to approach the window.

"Ronnie, what's going on?" Ricky asked, as he stood up.

"King is dead...We're walking out."

Ricky was still in shock from finding out about King's death the night before, and now the emotions of these students were running wild. This was a chance to be part of something truly important. Without another thought, Ricky ran to his brother. He climbed out of the window as fast as his chubby body could take him. Miss. Clay let it happen.

"Come on!" said Ronnie firmly.

Ricky and Ronnie ran to join the large crowd of people, which now included students leaving the front entrance of the elementary school. Ricky was the first of many of his classmates to climb out that window and be apart of something greater.

Officials in Detroit feared another riot, but by the grace of God and King's memory, the marchers remained mostly non-violent.

Detroit was no stranger to large crowds that year. A month later, Ricky and Ronnie were apart of an even bigger crowd of people that filled 12th Street. The morally concerned citizens gathering around a motorcade that inched its way toward Taylor Street, gentrified the pimps and prostitutes from their "spot." Standing tall on the back seat of the vehicle was presidential contender, Bobby Kennedy, whose campaign was welcomed by hundreds of Negroes, white reporters, and police officers in charge of "keeping order." The Negro citizens chanted his name, shook his hand, and touched him just to say they could. Ricky was one of those people. What struck Ricky the most was not the fact that he made physical contact with such a well renowned public figure, but how optimistic and happy Kennedy appeared that day. The way the sunshine bounced off his red hair, he in that instant represented this ray of light that illuminated the once dark 12th Street that had been subjected to a heinous riot just a year before. Although Ronnie related more to the Black Panther vision of racial equality, he could appreciate that a white man cared this much to come to this corner of the country and whose support for Civil Rights was unparalleled. A male civilian standing next to Ricky and Ronnie shook Kennedy's hand and was able to make eye contact with him.

"Stop the war. Bring us peace," said the Negro man.

Kennedy gave a decisive nod in that moment and let go of the man's hand.

Ricky took this comment in. Although at times he felt like he lived in a "war zone," he was actually in paradise compared to the bloody jungles of Vietnam. Ronnie thought of the unfairness of a Negro being treated like a second-class citizen at home, only to be drafted into a morally ambiguous war just to die and become another statistic.

Bobby Kennedy could end that war. Bobby Kennedy could change the world, thought Ronnie.

On June 5, 1968 the world did change, but not for the better. That morning, Wilma was feeling a bit more rested and for the first time in a long time, she actually made breakfast. When Ricky arrived in the kitchen he already saw Ronnie "chowing down" on some pancakes.

"Want some pancakes, Ricky?"

"Yeah with ice cream on top!" blurted out Ricky.

Ronnie almost choked on his food from laughing. Wilma gave her son a quizzical look before looking in the freezer.

"All out. Looks like you'll have to eat normally today."

Wilma made Ricky a plate with a stack of two golden brown flapjacks, with the traditional butter and maple syrup toppings. Ricky sat down at the table; grateful for his mother, cooking, but angry that the ice cream he saw Ronnie eating yesterday, was gone.

"Ronnie, you didn't save me any!"

"Like you need ice cream, fat boy," muttered Ronnie.

To avoid angering his mother by physically confronting Ronnie, Ricky thought of another way to get his revenge. Ricky got up and made his way to the television set. He turned it on to CBS so he could subject Ronnie to his least favorite show: *Captain Kangaroo*. But the scheduled morning children's show was not on. Instead the screen shone with news footage of reporters informing the audience that Bobby Kennedy was shot earlier that morning after winning the California Primary. The family watched in shock as they replayed the footage of Kennedy leaving the podium and cutting to chaotic imagery of him on the ground of the hotel kitchen. Ricky lost his appetite, Ronnie hated this broadcast more than *Captain Kangaroo*, and Wilma just stood silent as she burned one of the pancakes in her cast iron skillet.

"Not Bobby too. Why God?" Ricky questioned to himself.

Bobby Kennedy would die the next morning and so would the hopes and dreams of half the nation. King and Kennedy's deaths made 1968 a somber year for Detroiters. Ricky combated his sad feelings by finding refuge in cooking. He became quite the little chef by emulating his mother when she was home and experimenting on his own when she was "at work." Satisfying his family with his cooking gave Ricky the most joy.

The summer of 1968 yielded great new music, not just from Motown, but from all over the country. One song that was number one on the R&B singles chart for six weeks was James Brown's "Say It Loud—I'm Black and I'm Proud." The song was not only catchy, but also very important to how African Americans perceived themselves. A once uncomfortable word to describe one's race, was now made popular and cool. The term "black" no longer had a negative stigma but embodied a sense of pride. African Americans now associated themselves as "black" instead of "Negro." This shift in perspective became commonplace.

Although Ronnie's greatest joy was playing and listening to music, it was not James Brown's popular and thought provoking song that spoke to him that summer. A new album from The Jimi Hendrix Experience inspired Ronnie to emulate the band. While his peers all listened to the James Brown type funk and the soul music of Motown, Ronnie marched to a different beat by finding refuge in Rock. He along with the likes Bob Seger and Ted Nugent would perform at the "Open Mic Night" at The Glassdoor. This gave Ronnie the opportunity to finally show off his bongo playing talents from all the practicing he did at home, to the rest of his family's tolerance. With processed hair and beetle boots, Ronnie brought the whole club to life by the beat of his bongos.

Although Ricky and Ronnie had very different personalities, they both could relate to the abandonment of their respective fathers. Years ago, Wilma, Ronnie, and Ricky were out grocery shopping and as they were leaving, a funeral procession drove by. Wilma looked at her watch and nonchalantly told Ronnie that it was his father who was in the casket. Barney's alcoholism eventually led him to his death. Ronnie's estrangement with his father was so strong that he did not feel much of anything after Wilma told him that. He was actually more hurt from what he and Ricky saw that summer of '68.

It was a very hot day. The kind of day where sitting outside and eating ice cream seemed like the best way to cool off. It was the kind of day where newscasters joke about frying eggs on the concrete. And yet what Ricky and Ronnie gazed upon made their blood boil more than it already was. At first it was the recognizable car itself that drove in front of them as they sat on the stoop in front of their apartment. It was a white Chevrolet Impala, a car that was familiar to them growing up, especially Ronnie who had more vivid memories riding in it. Ronnie immediately thought of how his mother used to have a car just like that, before Jack took it. During their delirious daze from the heat, the boys saw a young man behind the wheel and a middle-aged man in the front seat. It wasn't until the man in the passenger seat pointed ahead and helped the driver steady the wheel, when Ricky and Ronnie realized that it was Jack.

"Dad?" asked Ricky as he snapped out his daze.

"What the fuck?" yelled Ronnie, as the car drove away.

The car that Jack stole from their mother the night of the kidnapping was now being used for what looked like driving lessons to some young teenager.

"Who was that boy?" asked Ricky.

"I think it's his new wife's son," replied Ronnie annoyingly.

Jack had not been around lately. Last time he was brought up was during an argument Wilma had with him on the phone regarding child support finances. Ronnie had a feeling Jack would never teach him how to drive nor give him a car. As much as Ronnie saw Jack as more of a father than Barney, it did not mean Jack saw Ronnie as his son. There was always a disconnect between the two and it usually left Ronnie jealous of the affection Jack gave Ricky. But in that moment even Ricky was left in the dust. Although Ricky was only 12 years old at the time, and driving was not yet on the horizon for him, he could not help but feel hurt to see the stepson spend that kind of quality time with his father.

Wilma had been an absentee parent herself in recent months due to the long nights she spent out. Whenever she did come home she was either tired, drunk, or both. Ricky would feed her and Ronnie would play her favorite Lena Horne record

for her. Whenever questioned about what she was doing outside

the home, Wilma would always respond with the same answer:

"I'm doing everything for you, boys."

The vague response satisfied Ronnie who would just nod

and go back to playing the bongos or tend to his pets, but Ricky

was not satisfied. He could see the pain behind his mother's eyes.

Whatever she was doing outside of the home, she hated. Ricky

did not like to see his mother like this. He had to find out what

she was doing.

If she wasn't doing hair, how was she spending her time?
thought Ricky.

A week later Ricky was only left with more questions and

curiosity when he witnessed his mother make a stop at another

apartment in the complex before coming home for the night. As

Ricky peered through the crack of the front door, he gazed upon

his mother giving a young black man a paper bag. Ricky almost

fell forward when he made the shocking realization that the

recipient of this mysterious delivery was his own cousin Bobby

Hunt. Bobby wore a red gabardine shirt that barely contained his stomach. He appeared more mean and rugged compared to the Bobby Hunt Ricky remembered from holiday dinners. No words were exchanged between Wilma and Bobby Hunt, which frustrated the anxious Ricky. Wilma turned toward her apartment and Ricky made sure he went back to his "dinner preparation" before Wilma came in. Of course the meal was already cooked and the table was already set. Wilma plopped down at the kitchen table. When Ricky approached her, he had every intention to confront her about what was in the paper bag but his mother looked too tired to talk.

"Thank you, baby. I love you," Wilma said to Ricky as she looked at the meal he made.

Wilma and Ricky embraced. The affection Ricky received in that moment meant more to him than what was in that paper bag.

Chapter 20: Fall 1969

The Detroit Tigers won the 1968 World Series but with the mass suburbanization of whites and blacks after the Civil Rights legislation and the riots, there weren't as many citizens celebrating within the city. It was almost like a ghost town with all of the businesses that packed up and moved or burned to the ground. With Bailey's Salon gone, Wilma had no reason to continue going to the Black Business Association meetings, contrary to Congressman Diggs pleas. A year after the Tigers victory, Wilma got in the groove of a new business venture. She was now making decent money, even if it wasn't the most conventional or morally acceptable way to do so.

Inside Shirley's apartment, Wilma and Shirley wore facemasks, rubber gloves, and white lab coats as they both mixed solutions in large bowls. Shirley studied Wilma, who was mixing at a very slow pace.

"What's wrong?" asked Shirley.

Shirley's inquiry snapped Wilma out of her fog, but she had no desire to delve into her feelings.

"Nothing," responded Wilma.

At the same time, Ricky was waiting on a bench on the corner of Linwood and Davison, soaked from the pouring rain. He held his large brown suitcase over his head as a shield from the drops, but getting wet was inevitable. Ricky managed to seek shelter by flagging down a cab. During his journey, Ricky placed the suitcase next to him and stared blankly out the window. The raindrops distorted the view of the urban backdrop and the newly released song, "Rainy Night In Georgia" by Brook Benton played appropriately on the radio. The somber song and the weary weather reflected Ricky's internal pain and it took every ounce of his being to stop himself from crying. Like his mother, he wanted to be strong.

Back at Shirley's apartment, Shirley continued badgering Wilma about sharing her feelings. As much as Shirley cared about Wilma, she still had a deadline to meet and quickly transferred the newly mixed powder into small packages and then into containers. Wilma continued stirring slowly and appeared to be daydreaming.

"What's going on with you? Spill it," demanded Shirley.

"I can't keep doing this to my kids," mumbled Wilma.

Shirley took this comment in. It was difficult for her to relate in that moment. Shirley did not have kids, nor planned to have any, especially now that she was closing in on her 50s. Jerry had once talked about adoption, but Shirley never thought she was cut out to be a mother. The satisfaction she got from accumulating her wealth was enough. It was this materialistic mindset that lead to a certain response.

"You're providing for them, Wilma."

It was almost as if Wilma did not hear Shirley's comment at all when she transitioned the topic of conversation to another family member of hers. One that wholeheartedly embraced the word: "indulge."

"Bobby is using. And I think he's selling to my relatives," said Wilma flatly.

"What makes you say that?"

"Bunny's husband wasn't acting like himself when I talked to him last week. I don't want my family using this shit.

It's bad enough I'm selling it."

Wilma's concerns were understandable. Shirley had seen what the product had done to young kids out on 12th Street. It was like the lights would be on but no one was home. Shirley never really had a moral compass, but she knew Wilma did. As Wilma sat down in a nearby wooden chair, Shirley decided to forget her deadline in that moment and console her best friend.

On the other side of town, a 16-year-old Ronnie stood in the foyer of the closed Floyd's Market. The loud sound of the pouring rain pounding on the rooftop was all Ronnie could hear but what he could see was exactly what he expected. He gazed upon his friend George Freeman running toward Ronnie in the foyer. George wore a blue jean jacket and matching jeans that had turned a darker blue color after being drenched from the rain.

"Fuck this weather," said George.

Ronnie was not one for small talk so he got right to the point.

"Get a pack from Bobby Hunt. We'll split it."

Ronnie proceeded to pull out a ten-dollar bill from his

pocket and handed it to George. Before George could say anything, Ronnie chimed in again with a very important demand.

"But don't say it's for me."

The last thing Ronnie wanted was for a family member of his to find out about such controversial behavior.

"Got it," retorted George decisively.

Ricky's cab stopped in front of a six-story apartment building. Ricky quickly ran out of the cab toward the front entrance, trying not to moisten his semi-dried clothing. He studied the intercom mounted on the wall outside the front door of the building. He found the button he was looking for and pressed it continuously.

A loud buzzer noise pierced the scene, which ruined Shirley's halfhearted consolation of a lethargic Wilma.

"Who the hell could that be?" muttered Shirley.

Shirley stoop up and approached the front door. She pressed the button on her respective intercom on the wall and spoke into it.

"Who is it?" asked Shirley curtly.

"Ricky. I need to talk to Mama."

The instant Ricky's voice was heard, Wilma stood up and ran to Shirley at the intercom. She gently pushed Shirley aside and pressed the button herself.

"I'm here, baby. Come on up."

Wilma buzzed him in. Once she turned to face Shirley, she realized how rude she had just been to her. But Shirley's concern was still for Wilma.

"So much for keeping your family away," said Shirley.

Back at Floyd's Market, Ronnie waited anxiously for his friend to return. George Freeman finally arrived and without saying a word, pulled out a small package from his pocket. He handed it to Ronnie and both of them cracked the biggest grins.

It's time to party, thought Ronnie.

There was a knock on the door of Shirley's apartment, which caused Wilma and Shirley to speed up their final transfers of the small packages to the larger containers. Once the supply was out of sight and out of mind, Wilma quickly opened the door.

She bent down and hugged a damp Ricky tightly.

"Baby, how did you get here?"

"Cab. I got an empty bag in the back seat."

"Why?" asked Wilma.

"So he thinks I'm bringing the money back down."

Wilma and Shirley made eye contact that revealed a level of surprise with Ricky's cleverness.

"Ricky you're pretty slick, John L. taught you well."

John L. was a name Wilma tried so hard to forget. Although John L. was a blood relative, that familial connection did not prevent him from betraying Wilma. Even if she could never prove it, she knew in her heart that he was behind the scam with Big Nick and Doreetha. The alcohol she consumed and her work with Shirley helped toward forgetting her cousin's existence, but Shirley's comment brought her rage right back to the forefront of her mind. Wilma snapped.

"Shut the fuck up, Shirley!"

"Let me know when you're ready," responded Shirley calmly and collectedly.

Shirley left the room, giving Wilma the privacy she desired with her son.

"You said you'd be back," said Ricky.

"Baby..."

Just as Wilma was about to explain, Ricky took command of the conversation. He needed to express his discontent with his situation.

"It's been three days, Mama! I'm hungry and there's nothing to eat at home."

Wilma had lost track of time. With all the mixing, packaging, and passing out she was doing, the hours and days blurred together. The moments in which Wilma did think of the well-being of her sons, she remembered there was plenty of food for Ricky to whip up with his budding culinary skills. But apparently that supply ran out. Wilma turned around to make sure that her work supplies were safely hidden and then reached into her pocket.

"I can't leave right now, baby. But here's a few dollars. Get some food for you and your brother. I'll be home tonight."

Ricky was not convinced. He stared at his mother and waited for her to say something else that would validate her previous statement. A certain phrase that, for Ricky, was like a blood oath.

"I promise," said Wilma sincerely.

At the foyer of Floyd's Market, Ronnie and George surveyed the area to make sure that no one could see them. Before George even told his "partner in crime" that the coast was clear, Ronnie opened the package and stuck his finger into the white powder. George turned around to see Ronnie place his finger up to his nose and take a deep sniff.

Brook Benton summed up the sentiments of the day perfectly for it did "seem like it was raining all over the world."

Later that night, Ricky and Ronnie sat on the couch physically together but mentally they were worlds apart. Ricky's interest was kept by the new television sitcom: *Julia*. Ricky related to that show by seeing the hardworking traits of his mother, embodied in the character of Julia, and as a loyal son, he could not help but see a little bit of himself in the character of

Corey. Ronnie was looking at the television set but wasn't processing any of the content. He could barely keep his head up. It was only until Wilma walked in, that he attempted to regain some of his lucidity. Ricky smiled at his mother who kept her promise.

"Mama, there's chicken in the kitchen," said Ricky.

"Thanks, baby. Hey, Ronnie."

Ronnie mumbled something incoherent and bobbed his head, without making eye contact with his mother.

"Tired?" asked Wilma as she moved closer to him.

Ronnie was unresponsive. She studied him intently and came to a terrible conclusion. One that she wanted to avoid at all costs. This was not tiredness it was a "dope nod." After all of the lessons and warnings she told her sons about alcohol and drug use, she could not believe that Ronnie could be so disrespectful and foolish. Her right hand began to shake, as the same kind of rage she felt when she heard her cousin's name, took over her body. She stared at the metal pencil sharpener on the table next to the couch for just a second before she swiftly grabbed it and slammed it against Ronnie's forehead. Ronnie did not even flinch but Ricky sure did. Ricky fell off the couch, fearful of his mother. It was the same kind of fear he felt when his father was around. Ronnie fell off the couch as blood gushed from his head. Wilma dropped the blood stained pencil sharpener, almost regretting what she had done. But then she realized this lesson taught to Ronnie was worth the pain she just inflicted. Her plan was to stop him from living a *life* full of pain.

"Now get your ass up so I can take you to the hospital."

An hour later, Ricky was leaning against the wall of a hospital room. He stayed on the opposite side of Wilma, with Ronnie sitting on an operating table in between them. A white doctor stitched up Ronnie's forehead as he was coming down from his high. This did not help with the pain but Ronnie sucked it up. A nearby nurse stood next to the doctor silently, holding a tray of supplies.

"I can't believe this shit," mumbled Wilma under her breath.

Ricky looked up at Wilma and their eyes met.

"Ricky, you believe this shit?"

Ricky examined his brother being stitched up and deduced that he could not believe that his mother could ever act so violently. Maybe she was not like Julia after all. Wilma then darted her gaze at Ronnie.

"I can't believe you," she said deplorably.

Ronnie looked at his fuming mother and put his head down. He had guilt for betraying his mother's trust, but he had no regrets in taking a substance that made him feel the best he had ever felt in his life.

"I can't believe you," said Wilma again as she shook her head in disgust.

The doctor finished up the stitching and put a large white bandage on Ronnie's forehead. Ronnie sighed with relief now that the deed was done. The doctor turned to Wilma, as he removed his latex gloves and placed them on the tray the nurse was holding.

"I gave him six stitches. Be sure to bring him back in a week to get them removed. You're done here."

"Thank you," replied Wilma.

The doctor nodded and exited the room. His departure was Wilma's cue to pull out her flask from her coat pocket and take a swig. Ricky stared at her, disappointingly. The nurse's face contorted before she uttered her one statement to Wilma.

"You can discharge him now."

Wilma took one more swig before putting her flask away. She stood still for a second to collect herself and then looked at Ricky and Ronnie.

"Let's go."

Ricky and Ronnie were both concerned when Wilma drove passed their home. The boys were not sure if this was a deliberate decision on the part of their mother or just a side effect of her drinking. Although Ronnie was in the doghouse, he decided to man up and ask what Ricky was too afraid to.

"Where are we going, Mama?"

"You'll see," said Wilma ominously.

Wilma parked in front of the police station. Ricky and Ronnie peered out at an establishment they had only seen embellished on the television. Their wonder transformed to confusion, which then became festered with fear. Wilma opened the back door and pulled Ronnie out of the car by his arm. Ronnie shrieked not because of the physical discomfort his mother was subjecting him to, but for the realization that he was about to be locked up like some criminal.

"Come on, Ricky," said Wilma as she dragged Ronnie to the entrance.

Ricky exited the car and walked slowly behind. Right as Wilma came in with Ronnie, Officer Lester was approaching the front counter. It had been a few years, but Lester could never forget the gorgeous Wilma Bailey. His pleasant demeanor from seeing Wilma was quickly dampened by the screaming boy next to her.

"Wilma Bailey. Where have you been?"

Wilma had no interest in forcing small talk with a man she would never see as a viable companion, even though he probably dreamed about her. She decided not to answer such a vague and pointless question and kept her response simple yet friendly.

"Hi, Lester."

Lester looked at the now shocked and silent Ronnie.

"What do you need, Wilma?"

"I want you to keep him here overnight."

"Huh? What? Mama!" yelled Ronnie, still trying to force his way out of his mother's iron grip. Wilma leaned in closer toward Lester.

"Let me know if he has a habit," whispered Wilma.

Lester was intoxicated by the smell of her shampoo and how smooth the words came out of those ruby red lips. This was the closest he had been to Wilma Bailey since dancing with her at Chubby's many moons ago and Lester liked it. He snapped out of it as she backed away. Lester then processed what Wilma actually wanted and then looked at her, skeptically. He decided to comply to her outlandish wish just in case it increased the chances of dating her.

"Anything for you, Wilma."

Lester signaled a nearby officer who approached Lester.

After Lester made his command softly, the officer proceeded to grab Ronnie, which was Wilma's cue to release her iron grip. The officer led Ronnie toward the back of the station. Ricky's eyes bulged as he watched his brother be taken away. Wilma smirked, as she was clearly proud of her decision.

"Mama, please! I'm sorry! Mama!"

"I'll be back tomorrow for you." yelled Wilma as Ronnie and the officer turned the corner. Wilma put her arm around a shocked Ricky and turned to exit. Ricky slowly slithered out from his mother's arm.

"Thank you, Les."

Lester nodded before Wilma and Ricky left the station. Wilma could see the fear in Ricky's eyes but it was necessary fear. She needed to convey that there were consequences for doing something as horrible as heroin. Amidst Wilma's disciplinary conviction, she felt a tinge of guilt. If she hadn't been selling these drugs in the streets with Shirley and Jerry then maybe Ronnie would have never desired the opportunity to get high.

What kind of a mother am I? thought Wilma.

A mother, who, like Shirley had said, was *providing for her sons.* The revenue Wilma was making was impressive and she knew that this dirty business would only be a means to an end once she became more financially stable.

"A means to an end," said Wilma softly.

"What, Mama?" asked Ricky from the back seat.

"Nothing, baby."

It was not nothing. It was a decision that would haunt Wilma Bailey the rest of her life.

Chapter 21: 1970

The holiday weekend was Wilma's first weekend that she had off in a long time. She used to have a lot of clients at the shop over the weekend and with her new "job" much of the buyers wanted their product on the weekends. Even though Mr. Silverman was Jewish, he respected the Christian holidays and let Wilma and Shirley enjoy their "drug free" weekend. It was the perfect time for Wilma to begin her annual spring-cleaning. Wilma organized her wardrobe by transferring folded clothing from her dresser drawers to her closet. Wilma hated wrinkles and made sure she had a lot of hangers for her different outfits. The nearby rotary phone rang and Wilma paused her domestic task to pick it up.

"Hello."

"Hi, Wilma. It's Ruby," said the soft-spoken lady on the other line.

Inside Ruby's kitchen, she sat at a table and smoked a cigarette.

"Hi, stranger. Happy Easter," said Wilma cheerfully as

she sat on her bed.

"It's only Friday," retorted Ruby.

Her comment and tone made it seem like Ruby did not want to celebrate the impending resurrection of Christ and instead dwell on the fact that he was crucified today.

"What's going on?" asked Wilma.

"I need your help."

The only kind of help Ruby ever sought out from Wilma had to do with cosmetology, which lead Wilma to respond to such a plea.

"I know it's a holiday weekend but I'm not doing any hair."

Ruby then took the conversation in a direction Wilma never expected.

"I'm pregnant, Wilma and I can't afford another baby."

Wilma was confused that of all people in her social circle, why she chose Wilma to tell this information. Wilma then recalled a service she had once done but chose not to mention because it was something she hated with a passion. Wilma deliberately played dumb.

"Why are you calling me?"

"Joanne told me you could help."

Her own sister sold her out. First John L. and his crew rob her blind, and now her own sister was giving out information that should never have been divulged. Wilma knew Joanne and Ruby were friends, but this was a line Wilma never expected her sister to cross.

"With her big ass mouth," said Wilma angrily.

Wilma's enraged comment about her sister had just revealed to Ruby that she could indeed help. Understanding that reality deflated Wilma emotionally.

"Please, Wilma," said Ruby desperately.

"I don't know, Ruby. I haven't done this in awhile."

"Please, Wilma. Please."

Ruby was scared. She was desperate and she was scared. She was also one of Wilma's most loyal clients and good friends. Even after Wilma had seared her neck years prior, Ruby still came back to Bailey's until it burned. Wilma pressed the receiver against her forehead, hard enough to make a red mark. She felt like breaking the phone with her iron grip before giving her response.

"Come to my house tomorrow with two hundred dollars. How many periods have you missed?"

"I think two."

Thank God, thought Wilma.

"Does your husband know?"

"Yes, he knows."

The husband's knowledge of the procedure was also another blessing and a crisis averted.

"I'll get the stuff. Come at one o'clock tomorrow," said Wilma decisively.

"I can't thank you enough, Wilma."

Ruby's tone was now upbeat and chipper while Wilma was now the one wallowing. She told herself she would never do this act again but out of friendship she decided to make an exception. An exception that would not be cheap.

"Don't forget the two hundred," said Wilma flatly.

Before Ruby could even respond, Wilma hung up the phone. She stood up and stared at one of the hangers on the bed. All she needed now was the rubber.

On Easter Sunday, Ricky and Ronnie played in the living room with their respective yo-yos as they waited for their mother to get ready for church. Ronnie embraced the role of big brother by teaching Ricky various tricks. A loud banging on the front door stopped the boys from playing for a second but it was not enough for them to stop completely. Wilma had taught them never to answer the door anyway.

From her bedroom, Wilma was able to peek through the window with curtains blocking her body. She gazed upon a short black man who she then remembered was Ruby's husband from an interaction she had with him at the shop years ago. The banging on the door persisted. Wilma left her bedroom and confronted her boys in the living room.

"Don't answer it," whispered Wilma loudly enough for her sons to hear, but soft enough for Ruby's husband not to be the wiser.

"We know, Mama," said Ricky.

"Wilma, please open up. Something's wrong with Ruby," yelled the husband to the door.

Wilma pressed her head up against the front door and contemplated what to do next. She had no desire to deal with this right now. She did the job and she wanted to have the day to repent and relax with her sons. Yet, her curiosity for Ruby's well-being got the best of her and she opened the door.

"What is it?" asked Wilma, skipping the pleasantries.

"She hasn't stopped bleeding," said the husband gravely.

For Wilma, receiving this information was like getting the wind knocked out of her.

I'm not Jesus. I can't heal. What the fuck is he doing here? thought Wilma.

She decided to tone down her actual verbal response.

"What are you doing here? Take her to a hospital."

"They're gonna ask me questions, Wilma. I don't know what to say."

Ruby's husband's nervousness and incompetence

frustrated her and what made her even angrier was contemplating the possibility of him disclosing Wilma's name or the procedure. She had to set him straight for both their sakes and especially Ruby's.

"Just get to her to a hospital now and don't mention my name."

Ruby's husband was clearly sad that Wilma could not or would not do more, but out of respect for Wilma, he complied with her wishes.

"I won't mention you, Wilma. I'm sorry I came here. Thank you."

He turned and walked away. Wilma slammed the door.

"I'm sick of this shit. God damn it, if this girl dies..." said Wilma to herself.

She ran her hands through her hair and looked at Ricky and Ronnie who had stopped playing the yo-yo and looked at their mother with pity.

"Hurry up and get dressed. We're late for the Easter Sermon," commanded Wilma.

As the boys retreated to their rooms, Ricky nudged Ronnie in order to tell him something.

"Ronnie, We gotta pray for Mama."

Ronnie nodded hesitantly. He still had some resentment toward his mother for the traumatic experience he had in jail. Although he was alone in his cell, it was one of the scariest nights of his life. This resentment would not stop Ronnie from praying for his mother though. He loved her in his own way, even if it did not seem as much as Ricky. Wilma Bailey needed all the prayers she could get.

That was the last "procedure" Wilma Bailey had done. There was something eerie about doing it on a High Holy Day that made Wilma vow she would never perform one again. A few months had passed and Wilma honored that promise.

It was now the fall of 1970 and nature's beautiful leaves contrasted the animosity Wilma felt on one of those autumn nights. The kids were enjoying themselves though. Ricky and Cousin Bobby Hunt watched as Ronnie played the bongos enthusiastically. He dominated The Glassdoor over the summer and seemed to be dedicating his whole life to music. As much as Wilma was proud of Ronnie for living his dream, she did fear that he would not make a decent living. Now as a 17-year-old, adulthood came knocking on Ronnie's door. He had been hesitant to answer. As Ronnie reached his own version of a crescendo, Wilma came into the living room from the kitchen. A thought had crossed her mind that needed to be addressed.

"Did you get the mail?" yelled Wilma to Ronnie.

Ricky and Bobby Hunt turned toward Wilma from the couch but Ronnie continued playing, obliviously. He kept his eyes closed when he played which, had apparently helped with his "rhythm." Like his mother when she was his age, he wanted to avoid the chance of seeing a "sour face" to throw him off.

"Put the damn bongos down!" yelled Wilma loudly.

Ronnie opened his eyes and saw his mother staring at him coldly. He quickly stopped playing, obeying his mother.

"Did you check the mail?" Wilma repeated firmly.

"Yeah," said Ronnie softly.

"Was the check in there?"

Ronnie simply shook his head no. Jack had done terrible things in the past but this ongoing disregard for his son, made Wilma the angriest.

"That son of a bitch can't even send fifteen a week for his own son," murmured Wilma to herself.

Wilma walked right over to her liquor cabinet and pulled out her loyal companion who compensated her everyday; a bottle of Seagram's gin. She poured herself a shot and downed it faster than her kids had ever seen. Bobby Hunt had always gravitated toward Wilma over Jack, and he saw this situation as an opportunity to "knock Jack down a peg" and help his cousin out.

"I have an idea, Wilma."

It was an idea that was composed of pathos with a tinge of manipulation, typical of Bobby Hunt. Since his move to Detroit, his moral compass took him in a more corrupt direction. Much like his cousin John L., he believed that the conventional ways to make money were not geared toward African Americans. The workplace was still dominated by white people with their own versions of racism, no matter how subtle. Like Wilma's, Bobby

Hunt's business was drugs, which made them co-workers. It instilled fear in Wilma when Bobby Hunt would bring up his "ideas" in front of the children. He usually kept it appropriate, but one could never know with Bobby Hunt. Wilma was doubtful of Bobby Hunt's idea but she figured it would be more effective than her current methods.

A couple hours later, Bobby Hunt drove Wilma, Ricky and Ronnie in his blue 1970 Oldsmobile Tornado. It was a car that Bobby Hunt loved more than life itself and one that the kids pretended was a submarine, navigating the deep blue waters of the city. Wilma was indifferent and kept thinking whether she should abort this mission. They pulled up in front of a two-story brick bungalow on Murray Hill. The porch light shined brightly, giving them a clear view of the beautiful home. From the passenger seat, Wilma turned to the back seat to address her son.

"Okay, Ricky. Go up to the porch, ring the doorbell, and get your money."

"All right, Mama."

Ricky exited the car and walked slowly up to the porch.

As he escalated the stoop, he turned back around and looked into his mother's anxious eyes. As much as he did not want to do this, he wanted to make his mother happy. He turned back around to face the door and rang the doorbell. Ricky and the rest of his family waited with bated breath. Half a minute had passed and Ricky was tired of waiting. Wilma kept her eyes moving, darting her vision to the different windows of the house. The curtain behind the right side window of the house moved slightly, indicating to Wilma that someone inside saw Ricky and the car. Instead of the door opening like they hoped, the porch light went out. Ricky lowered his head, knowing he was not going to make his mother happy this evening. He turned and walked back to the car, slamming the door behind him.

"Bright idea, Bobby. Can you please take us home?" scolded Wilma.

"Okay, Wilma," replied Bobby Hunt meekly.

Ricky shed a tear. He was not going to get the child support money he deserved and his own father had no desire to see him.

Chapter 22: 1972

Detroit had lost the glamour and economic potential that it had a decade before. Suburbanization ran rampant with African Americans following the white people out of the city. Berry Gordy Jr. was one of them. In 1972, he officially moved his famous record label; Motown to Los Angeles leaving many Detroiters dissatisfied and betrayed. To add insult to injury, Detroit was denied its seventh bid to host the Summer Olympics, making it the city with the most unsuccessful attempts to be the epicenter of healthy and friendly competition. The businesses sure as hell were not competing either. Mr. Silverman's business venture however was flourishing.

Inside his large Sherwood Forest Mansion, Mr. Silverman walked down the long white tiled hallway. His dress shoes clattered and echoed through the home. At a large brown door stood Moe with his arms crossed. He appeared as if he was guarding a palace entrance or something. Mr. Silverman approached him.

"I'm gonna talk to Wilma right now but I'll meet up with

you later," said Mr. Silverman.

Moe nodded and turned to walk away. He always appreciated the shorter exchanges.

"Wait," interjected Mr. Silverman.

Moe turned back around and raised his eyebrows, conveying his curiosity.

"Who did that concert at Masonic Temple last night?"

"I'm not sure," retorted Moe.

"Did we even get a piece of that?"

Mr. Silverman's tone became more firm after Moe answered his question with a subtle shrug.

"Please, fuckin' find out before Hoffman does."

Moe did his classic head nod to show his understanding and exited the mansion. Mr. Silverman opened the brown door to his den and shut it behind him. Mr. Silverman gazed upon his guest, Wilma Bailey sitting upright on the edge of a couch next to the fireplace. Without saying a word, Mr. Silverman waltzed to the other side of the room to his turntable on the counter of the bar. "I Pagliacci: The Sad Clown" by Luciana Pavorotti played in the background which complemented Wilma's internal state perfectly. He took out a couple glasses from the cabinet.

"A drink?" he asked.

Wilma hesitated. All she craved in that moment was alcohol. She knew it would dull the pain she was currently feeling. She watched anxiously as Mr. Silverman poured his own.

"No," Wilma said softly.

Wilma was about to give her boss some bad news and making sure she was in full control as she explained, was a top priority.

"Right answer. I like you better sober."

Wilma gave a half smile before uttering the brutal truth.

"I don't have all the money," she said flatly.

"What are you talking about?" asked Mr. Silverman calmly.

"I'm five grand short."

Mr. Silverman coughed deeply after taking a sip. This was not good news at all.

"What the hell happened, Wilma?"

Wilma sighed, knowing he needed an explanation, but she had barely enough strength to speak about it.

"I went over to Bobby's friend's house to get the money and give him the package."

As Wilma told Mr. Silverman the anecdote, she relived it in her head. Wilma knocked on the door of the flimsy apartment door that seemed to be hanging from one hinge. Bobby Hunt opened the door swiftly and let her cousin in. Wilma took in the messy apartment that reeked of body odor and cigarettes. She knew she was going to meet Bobby's friend but was still startled to see the 28-year-old as he rounded the corner from the kitchen. He was a tall, slender, black man, who studied Wilma from head to toe. He sniffled his nose continuously and kept his eyes on his new houseguest as if she was somehow a threat to him getting his next fix. He was the true embodiment of what it meant to be a "dope fiend." Wilma broke eye contact once Bobby Hunt put his hand on her shoulder.

"About time you got here," said Bobby Hunt snidely.

"Who the hell is your friend?" asked Wilma has she

returned her gaze to the "dope fiend."

"This is *my* place," he responded proudly, as if claiming the land of filth to be one's own was something to be proud of.

"You got my money?" asked Wilma, as she turned toward Bobby Hunt.

Bobby Hunt nodded anxiously yet did not indicate where the money was, not with words nor body language. This was unsettling for Wilma.

"Where's the bathroom?" she asked.

The dope fiend friend pointed to a hallway.

"I'll be right back," said Wilma.

Wilma made her way to a bathroom that looked like it had not been cleaned in years. Mildew and dirt were the main tenants. She closed and locked the door behind her. She took out a few small packages containing white substances from her purse and placed them on the sink counter. Before she could even process her next move, the door was slammed open abruptly, breaking the lock. The dope fiend friend pressed his revolver against Wilma's head as she was forced onto the toilet seat. Bobby Hunt walked in slowly behind him. Once Wilma had looked into the eyes of Bobby Hunt, she could tell that the fun loving cousin she had grown to love, was gone. Bobby Hunt was no longer a drug dealer but a junkie, who was a slave to his own supply. Dope had morphed her cousin as it clearly did the same to his friend, who now held her life in his erratic hands.

"Take your fucking clothes off, Wilma. I don't have time to play," commanded Bobby Hunt viciously.

Bobby Hunt then proceeded to take the packages and stuff them in his deep pockets. Once he realized Wilma was still in shock and unmoving, he decided to change his tone to be a little bit more threatening.

"Now!" he yelled.

She was not afraid to die in that instant. Death seemed like a welcomed release from the hell that her life had become. She almost decided not to comply with such an atrocious command, but she thought of Ricky and Ronnie. Her boys needed their mother and Wilma Bailey was not about to lose her life over some drugs. She began to strip as she started to breathe heavily.

The dope fiend friend still kept his gun pushed up to her temple, as he stared menacingly at her. Snot ran from his nose onto his lips and he proceeded to lick the draining mucous. Wilma was now naked and shivering. Bobby stuffed all of her clothes into a garbage bag, which was something Wilma did not expect, but then again, the whole visit was not what she had expected.

"Let's go," said Bobby Hunt to his dope fiend friend.

The dope fiend friend released his gun from Wilma's head but still kept it pointed at her.

"Don't come out of this bathroom until we're gone," commanded Bobby Hunt.

Bobby Hunt placed the garbage bag over his shoulder and he and his dope fiend friend left the bathroom and the apartment.

As Wilma finished telling Mr. Silverman the story, she put her head in her hands and became hysterical.

"I sat on the cold fucking toilet naked for a half hour. I was afraid to come out the god damn bathroom."

Mr. Silverman's face perfectly expressed his mixed emotions of sympathy and rage. It was clear that on Wilma's face, rage was the emotion that suddenly took her over.

"I want you to kill them mother fuckers!"

Wilma thought back to the first time she went to the racetrack with Mr. Silverman. That was when she first seriously considered the potential of this man killing someone. She knew he had the power to exact her version of revenge on her cousin and his "partner in crime." She waited with bated breath for him to respond to her request. Mr. Silverman took a long sip from his glass. Unlike Wilma, drinking made Mr. Silverman think more clearly.

"You're fucking done. I'm gonna get you a job. It's over, Wilma."

This answer did not satisfy Wilma, whose emotions were running very high.

"No, I want you to kill them motherfuckers."

"I Pagliacci: The Sad Clown" faded out as Wilma uttered her demand again.

"The shit they're using will do that. Don't worry about them anymore. Wilma, you're done," said Mr. Silverman sternly.

Mr. Silverman walked across the room to a canvas painting of Pagliacci hanging on the wall above the fireplace. Mr. Silverman took the painting off of the wall, which revealed a safe behind it. He put in the combination, opened it, and pulled out a stack of cash. He closed the safe, walked over to Wilma, and placed the money on the table in front of her.

"I'll cover it. Meet me at the cleaners tomorrow at 10 A.M. Don't be late."

Wilma came to her senses. She knew killing Bobby Hunt and his friend would not erase the memory that was now branded into her brain. And as much as she hated how her family members had treated her, she would never approve of the death of a blood relative. She processed Mr. Silverman's gesture and stood up to hug Mr. Silverman tightly.

"Thank you," said Wilma.

Wilma shed a single tear as she nuzzled her head in Mr. Silverman's shoulder. Besides her father when he was sober, Mr. Silverman was the only man in her life that made Wilma feel safe and protected.

"Don't thank me, Wilma. We'll work out a payment plan."

But as much as Mr. Silverman made her feel secure, he was still a businessman, who valued wealth over people. Wilma needed to accept that, although, she could have sworn she saw glimpses of purity in Mr. Silverman's heart. She would continue to look for them.

The next morning, Mr. Silverman and Wilma entered Silverman's Cleaners together. The place was empty which made Mr. Silverman's welcome tour less chaotic.

"This is where you'll be working."

Mr. Silverman gestured his hand to a long beige counter stretching from one end of the building to the other. A dozen leather chairs were lined up in front of the counter.

"Wait here," said Mr. Silverman.

Wilma sat down in one of the chairs and examined her new workspace. It was definitely bigger than her salon, which at first was exciting to her until she thought of how impersonal the job could be.

"I'm gonna get your paperwork together. I'll be right back," said Mr. Silverman.

Wilma nodded which served as Mr. Silverman's cue to walk across the room to a large brown door with a glass mirror. Inside Mr. Silverman's office, was Mr. Hoffman seated at Mr. Silverman's desk, pulling rank once again. This act did not bother Mr. Silverman like it did in years passed. He had more tangible things to worry about rather than who was sitting at his desk. Moe was seated at front of the desk, and turned to face Mr. Silverman upon his entry.

"So that's the infamous Wilma Bailey," said Mr. Hoffman ominously.

He peered out the mirror on the office door, which was actually a two-way mirror in which the men could see Wilma but she could not see them. Mr. Silverman had this installed because he always enjoyed keeping an eye on the day-to-day tasks of his business, without his staff ever knowing when he was looking.

"I'm making Wilma a counter girl here," said Mr. Silverman firmly yet with a tinge of nervousness in his voice.

"You want her working here? Are you doped up right now?" asked Mr. Hoffman incredulously.

Mr. Silverman did not want to give up that easily.

"Look," interjected Mr. Silverman.

"No, you look, Max. Her shop worked well for policy but that burned. She got scammed by that nigger Nick fucker. She's a liability."

Mr. Silverman lowered his head to gather his thoughts. If only he had some alcohol left in his office.

"Do you know who's been peddling your heroin for the past five years?" asked Mr. Silverman.

This was the most confrontational he ever got in front of his boss but to him Wilma Bailey was worth it, to a certain extent, of course.

"Wilma, Shirley, Jerry, and all those other niggers out there. Why should she get special treatment?"

Mr. Silverman tried to think of a response that Mr. Hoffman could relate to and still manage to tell the truth.

"Her head's been at the end of a gun barrel too many

times. She deserves peace."

"What about her last batch?" asked Mr. Hoffman.

Mr. Silverman pulled out a money roll, held together with a rubber band. He placed the money on the desk in between Mr. Hoffman and Moe. Moe stood up and started counting the money as Mr. Hoffman and Mr. Silverman glared at each other.

"It's all here," said Moe defiantly.

"I'm glad it is, for her sake," said Mr. Hoffman.

Moe felt it would be good to ease the tension in the room by changing the subject.

"Oh, before I forget. You know that concert at Masonic that we didn't get a piece of?"

"Yeah..." said Mr. Silverman.

"They're the same motherfuckers that outbid us on the Old Playboy Club."

Mr. Silverman had been hoping Moe would come to him with this information first so they could figure out a way to present the information to Mr. Hoffman in a less intrusive way. Moe was not always the brightest, but he did wash all of the dirty laundry that Hoffman and Silverman had no desire to do.

"Sounds like some fuckers who don't know their place," said Mr. Hoffman fumingly.

"The organization is called Progressive 11 and you'll never guess who runs it?"

"Who?" asked Mr. Hoffman while Mr. Silverman just stared at Moe, hoping it was not someone he knew personally.

"You won't fucking believe it."

Although Moe was always serious, he did sometimes bask in moments of drama.

"Damn it just tell us," said Mr. Silverman.

"Wilma's fucking husband Jack."

Mr. Silverman's face dropped. All three men looked at Wilma sitting at the counter through the two-way mirror at the same time. Moe smirked, Mr. Hoffman glared, and Mr. Silverman watched her with a wave of concern that he made sure to keep internal.

"You're right, Max. She should be working here," said Mr. Hoffman darkly.

Later that day, Ricky was in bed, throwing a tennis ball at the ceiling and then catching it. He enjoyed finding that balance where he could still catch it without the ball going too far in front of him. He was also quite bored. A knock on his door broke up the monotony.

"Come in."

Wilma stumbled into his room, clearly drunk. Ricky glanced at her and processed her drunkenness. He chose not to acknowledge her and continued tossing the ball.

"You know I want what's best for you. Don't you, baby?"

Then stop drinking, Mama, thought Ricky.

"I know, Mama," said Ricky betraying his thoughts yet honoring his mother.

"I'm not going to be making as much money anymore. Ronnie's gonna be starting at Job Corps now..."

Wilma's sentence was not complete. It was if she forgot how to finish what she wanted to say. Ricky had a hard time discerning whether it was the alcohol making her forgetful or if she was deliberately hesitating to tell him something.

"I need you to live with your father."

Ricky failed to catch the falling ball. Ricky's relationship with his father was estranged to say the least. It was all downhill after he kidnapped him but then it was Jack's blatant disrespect and absence that served as the metaphorical nails in the coffin when it came to Ricky's dismissal of such a man.

"Why him? Why can't I live with Aunt Joanne?"

This was a valid question. One that Wilma Bailey had asked herself. But Wilma thought it was time to bury the familial hatchet.

"You need to have a relationship with your father."

"I don't want to."

Ricky's stern demeanor was surprising for Wilma to see. Although he was only 15 years old, Wilma had just caught a glimpse of Ricky as a strong man, one that stayed true to his values and convictions. She could not blame Ricky for his aversion to live with a man who showed little support for him over the years, but her decision was more reflective of her financial situation.

"Then do it for me, baby. Once I start making more money, I'll have you move back."

Ricky could see the desperation in his mother's eyes. Ricky almost suggested getting a job to pay for his rent but he worried about finding that balance between work, school, and football. He decided then and there to comply with his mother's wishes.

"All right, Mama. I'll do it."

Wilma kissed a reluctant Ricky on the forehead. She got up slowly from Ricky's bed and meandered out, paying close attention to her footing. Ricky looked over at his bookshelf and stared at the only Christmas gift his father had given him: a piggy bank. The symbolism of the gift, only served as a painful reminder to Ricky of how much Jack had stolen from his mother. Living with this type of man was going to be interesting to say the least, but what excited Ricky was the chance to poke his father with subtle remarks so he could remind him of the pain he had inflicted. Maybe, just maybe, a resolution was possible.

A few months later, a copper 1972 Chevrolet Impala

pulled into the driveway of Jack's Murray Hill House. Jack and Ricky exited the vehicle with Ricky holding a suitcase. Ricky glanced at the porch light, which reminded him of being left out in the cold. They approached the front door as a white neighbor strolled down his driveway to pick up his newspaper.

"Hey, Jack," he said.

Jack smiled and waved. Ricky raised his eyebrows. He had never lived this close to white folk before, at least not white folk that appeared to be this friendly. Ricky wondered in that instant how much of living in a predominately white neighborhood had curbed Jack's racism. Ricky was not ready to get that deep with his father, as forcing small talk with the man was hard enough. The men entered the living room and Jack made their presence known.

"We're home."

Edna walked into the living room. She wore an apron that represented the domestication that Jack always wanted in Wilma.

"Took you long enough," she said snottily.

"Hi," said Ricky.

Edna ignored Ricky, which was a clear indicator that he was not welcomed in her eyes.

This will be fun, thought Ricky sarcastically.

"The guys are downstairs waiting on you," said Edna as she fixed Jack's wrinkled collar.

"Thanks, Edna. Can you show Ricky his room, please?"

Jack not only wanted his wife and his son to cultivate a relationship, but the business in the basement was more of a priority than getting his son situated. He figured it was a "woman's job" anyway. Edna complied by nodding slowly, giving Jack the green light to go downstairs. His remodeled basement was filled with a seven-foot slate pool table. Crowding around the beautiful console were a dozen middle-aged African American men, sipping on their respective glasses. Jack's friend and co-worker, Benny, broke the pool balls as his comrade Carl acknowledged Jack's arrival.

"There he is."

Keith, another colleague, asked the question on everyone's mind.

"Where have you been, Jack?"

"Picked up my son."

"Dave?" asked Carl.

"No, man. My real son, Ricky."

"You think he's gonna be okay, Jack?" asked Carl concernedly.

"Now that he's with me," said Jack firmly.

Jack grabbed a pool stick from the wall mount and made his shot after Benny scratched.

"I was just telling the guys that we need to be careful moving forward," said Benny cautiously.

"Progressive 11 is all about progress, am I right, guys?" said Jack jokingly.

The guys nodded and mumbled to themselves. Benny tended to be a "worrywart" and sometimes projected weakness onto the company Jack created. Jack always liked to diffuse the fear that fumed out of Benny, especially if humor could be incorporated.

"But with prices going up and the mob breathing down

our neck, I don't know what we're gonna do."

Some of the guys appeared concerned and looked to their boss for assurances. As much as Benny tended to worry, he did have a point. Their unstable financial situation coupled with the mob's territorial mentality was threatening. Jack wanted to assure his colleagues with a logical and rational point but one could not come to him in time. He decided that appearing vigilant and strong was the way to go.

"I only fear God."

Jack made a shot and got two in a pocket.

Later that night, Ricky was lying on a single bed in a small bedroom. He was bummed that he forgot to pack his tennis ball, not just to toss around, but as a reminder of his loyal friend, Blackie.

"Hey, baby," said Edna, outside the bedroom.

Ricky got up and opened the door a crack. He saw his father kiss Edna, which made him nauseous.

"How was the meeting?" she asked.

"Fine. They're gone."

Jack glanced at Ricky's face, partially revealed through the crack of the door.

"What are you doing in there?" asked Jack angrily.

Ricky got nervous, knowing that he was just caught spying. Ricky opened the door all the way and shrugged. Jack's anger was not actually directed at Ricky for spying but toward Edna.

"I thought I told you I wanted him to stay in the upstairs room."

"When family comes to town they always stay up there. I don't want guests staying next to us."

"My son needs his privacy. He's living here too," said Jack assertively.

No matter how good Edna thought her reasoning was, she was not going to win this argument. She rushed into the bedroom and picked up Ricky's suitcase. She erratically threw it down the hallway and shrieked crazily.

"What the fuck is wrong with you?" asked Jack loudly, to match the decibel level of her unnecessary shriek. Jack advanced toward Edna but Ricky stood in the way.

"Dad, it's okay. I don't want any problems."

Ricky picked up his suitcase and put back some of the clothes that came out. Although Jack did not know Ricky all too well, he respected him a lot for that reaction. He was more mature than he had originally thought. Jack did have a moment where he reflected on the kind of father he had been. It was the kind of reflection Ricky wanted his father to have. Despite Ricky's desire to hear paternal consolation, Jack's pride would never allow him to convey such emotional sentiment. What had came out of his mouth was the most heart warming thing he could think of while projecting himself as a strong masculine figure.

"Okay, son. Welcome home."

Chapter 23: 1974

1974 was an important year for the city of Detroit. After the gas crisis that had occurred a year prior, Detroit tried hard to find its footing with regards to reinvigorating the auto industry. With the price of gas prices sky high, foreign vehicles became the cheaper and more popular option. A new and fresh face emerged in politics, one that represented hope to many of the African Americans that had been beaten and battered financially and emotionally by consumer suburbanization. The once owner of Young's Barbecue, Coleman Young, ran for mayor and was elected in 1974. His plan to help the auto industry was to approve the construction of two new plants: The General Motors Detroit/Hamtramck Assembly Plant, also known as "Poletown" for its location in a primarily polish neighborhood and Chrysler Jefferson North Assembly Plant. But these developments would take time and that was not a luxury the citizens of Detroit had.

Wilma's old boss, Doris was one of those people. In 1974 she was now 80 years old and she definitely played the part. Her face had more substantial wrinkles and she utilized a cane as her support system. The old woman entered Silverman's Cleaners wearing a purple coat that stood out amongst the patrons. Wilma Bailey along with six younger girls stood at the counter making their transactions with the customers. Doris hobbled over barely able to hold her own bag of clothing. Although she was elderly, she still had her wits about her and never forgot a face. When her and Wilma made eye contact, Doris was the first to establish familiarity.

"Wilma? Wilma Bailey is that you?"

"Doris!"

Wilma walked over and hugged Doris tightly. Seeing Doris was like a breath of fresh air for Wilma. It reminded her of pleasant times working in her small shop, honing her cosmetic talents. It seemed like a different lifetime. The memories that came into her mind were fond in that instant yet her emotional state got weaker once Doris brought up a different memory.

"I saw your shop burning on TV. I prayed every day for you, Wilma."

Wilma's cheerful demeanor was seriously dampened but

she managed to address her goodwill.

"Thank you, Doris."

"Wilma, don't tell me all those fake wigs stopped you from doing hair?"

Doris was partially right. Between all of the synthetic wigs, salons like what Bailey's once was, were almost nonexistent now. The consumer market was dwindling. As much as Wilma Bailey wanted to open a new salon, she knew it would not be profitable, even if Mr. Silverman invested in it. Wilma decided to lie to Doris to avoid any deeper discussion of why in fact she was working at Silverman's Cleaners.

"I just needed a change."

"How are Ronnie and Ricky?"

"They're fine..."

Just as Wilma was about to talk about the specifics of how her sons were doing, Doris interrupted.

"Wilma, last time I got my clothes back the buttons were off my pant suits. Can you take care of my clothes and do them right?"

In that moment, Wilma was relegated from "old friend" to "worker bee." She wanted nothing more than to catch up with the wise old woman but Doris did not seem as interested. It seemed that the idea of friendship had become a foreign concept to Wilma Bailey.

"Yes, Doris. I will."

Doris handed Wilma the bag of clothes.

"Make sure now, Wilma."

Doris leaned on her cane and slowly exited the building.

"Fuckin' bitch," mumbled Wilma, under her breath.

All the counter girls laughed. At least Wilma could still make some people happy.

Chapter 24: 1976

During the spring of 1976, Ricky was 19 and working as an attendant at the Clark Service Station on Conant and Nevada. On a warm spring afternoon, sweating in his dark blue jump suit, Ricky swept the pavement around the gasoline pumps. His boss, Mr. Rice, had an almost OCD outlook when it came to the outside appearance of his business. If there was one thing he hated more than anything, it was litter. Ricky found it comical considering Mr. Rice's business of burning fossil fuels did more damage to the environment than littering ever could. Ricky humored Mr. Rice's obsession for sweeping because it meant getting some fresh air and increased the possibility of seeing a familiar face on the road that may or may not stop for some gas. The driver of a shiny black Galaxie 500 Convertible, that had just pulled into the station, was more than just a familiar face, he was family.

"Oh shit, you ain't chubby no more!" said a tall and slender Ronnie as he exited the vehicle.

Between living in separate homes and living different

lives, Ricky and Ronnie hadn't seen each other in months. In that time Ricky had turned a lot of his fat into muscle. For the first time in Ronnie's life, he said Ricky wasn't chubby. It felt weird yet nice to hear.

"Hey Ronnie!"

Ricky dropped the broom and approached Ronnie.

"Give me five on the black hand side," commanded Ronnie lightheartedly.

Just as Ronnie raised his hand to do their classic hand move, Ricky interjected.

"Stop playing, boy."

Ricky gave Ronnie a warm embrace instead.

"Making a little money, huh?" asked Ronnie.

Ronnie accentuated the word "little." Ricky caught the inflection.

"Wish it was as much as you. Looks like Chrysler is treating you nice."

Ricky's gaze went right to the beautiful piece of machinery that sat in front of them. He almost laughed to himself when he remembered how he and Ronnie were both jealous of Edna's son, Dave driving the Impala. Now Ronnie was driving a much better car. It was a car he deserved after all of the hardships he experienced in his life.

"I'm telling you, Ricky. Job Corps is the way to go. Better than all that college bullshit."

Ronnie was never the best student in school. It was less about having low intelligence and more of just lacking the motivation for pursuing a conventional and intellectual occupation. Since higher education was never a real possibility for him, it was easier to call such academic pursuits "bullshit" and promote his vocational school, centering on automotive technical training. Ronnie finally put his childhood dream to be a Veterinarian to rest and decided to mirror the one strong male figure he had in his life by working on cars. Ricky however had no intention to be like Jack and instead preferred Ronnie's idea of "slinging bullshit."

"I still wanna give Ann Arbor a try."

Ronnie put his pride aside for he was proud of his brother

in that moment. He always admired Ricky for his tenacity and to even mention Ann Arbor as being a possible next step, made Ronnie happy. He still could not get over Ricky's physical transformation and then remembered that a certain sport Ricky had been playing must have been a factor.

"I heard you was playing football," said Ronnie.

"Yeah I was playing at Pershing."

From Wilma's constant praise of Ricky's football involvement and good grades, sometimes the line between jealousy and admiration was blurred for Ronnie. But what was not blurry was Ronnie's anger toward Ricky for not inviting him to a certain milestone moment.

"Why didn't you send me an invitation to your graduation?"

"Because I didn't go."

"What? Why?" asked Ronnie sternly.

"All I asked from Jack was a new suit. He didn't give me one, so I didn't go."

"What's wrong with you?"

"After all those years that's the only thing I asked for. Edna talked him out of it."

Edna definitely influenced Jack's decision quite a bit. In fact, when Ricky had asked his father in his bedroom, Edna rose up out of bed swiftly, like the possessed girl from *The Exorcist*, and put in her "two cents" which entailed that, since Ricky would be wearing a gown, a new suit would not be visible, thus an unnecessary investment. This response had been appalling for Ricky due to the fact that this was the only thing he had ever asked his father for and he could not even get that. Edna's only suggestion was for Jack to get him a new pair of shoes. As Ricky was internally reliving the family drama, Ronnie was getting angry with Ricky for his excusive answer.

"Look, fool. That was a place for you to stay so you could graduate."

"I still graduated, I just didn't go to the ceremony. Ended up singing on the corner drinking some Wild Irish Rose for the first time with Carl Marley and Spud."

"Don't be drinking that shit, it'll kill you," joked Ronnie.

"Yeah, I know but I'm done with Jack, man," said Ricky.

"The only reason he picked you up that day was because he owed 28,000 dollars in back child support."

"How you know that?"

"Cause Mama signed off on it."

Ricky knew that his relationship with his father wasn't the closest, but to think that the financial reasons for his extended stay outweighed the desire to reconnect with his son, stung.

"Wow. Ain't that a bitch. No wonder I felt like a guest the whole time I was there."

"Where are you now?"

"Down the street with Mama until college in the fall."

"She still drinking?"

"Not so much every day but still a lot on the weekends. I'm dealing with it."

"Isn't that all we do? Deal with shit."

Such a statement really made Ricky reflect. In that moment, he stood in front of someone he knew and loved his whole life; a person he watched grow from a rambunctious teenager to a man supporting himself on his own. Despite all of the terrible events they went through and all of the pain they felt, Ricky could find solace in the fact that he and Ronnie dealt with it and managed to find strength from it. Ricky instantly wished his mother could find that same kind of strength.

How much more could her liver take? thought Ricky.

Ricky's stream of consciousness met the metaphorical rock that was Ronnie's next comment.

"Just thought I'd stop by. I'm gonna come pick your ass up on Friday and we're gonna do something."

"You always say that shit," said Ricky in a joking tone.

Ricky was hoping this time Ronnie would respond to his sarcastic comment and convey a little validation that he indeed was going to pick Ricky up on Friday. Alas, Ronnie just waved and jumped into his vehicle before driving away. Ricky picked up the broom and continued sweeping the pavement. Just as he thought his mindless task was over, he glanced at a piece of trash right where Ronnie's car was parked. He swept up the small plastic bag without a second thought. What Ricky didn't realize was that the bag had a small portion of a substance that had plagued the youth of Detroit for almost a decade. It was a substance that Ronnie once tried and, despite getting bashed in the head with a pencil sharpener, could not stay away from. Ricky's concerns for his mother's health were far less immediate than his concerns for Ronnie should have been. Hindsight will always be 20/20.

That same evening, Jack, Benny, and a few other black men exited the Chevrolet Gear & Axle building together after a long day of work. They waved each other off as Jack approached his Impala. From the other side of the parking lot, sat Moe in his Electra. He watched Jack like a hawk, floating over its prey. Just as Jack opened his driver door was when Moe got out of his vehicle and walked briskly toward him.

"Excuse me, are you Jack?"

If there was one thing Jack did not take kindly to it was an ambush.

"Who the hell are you?"

"A friend," said Moe nonchalantly.

Jack looked Moe up and down. He knew he looked familiar but could not place his finger on when he gazed upon such a strange and mysterious looking white man.

"Me and some fellas I work with have been admiring your new organization..."

Jack raised his eyebrows conveying a level of surprise with a tinge of suspicion.

"Progressive 11," stated Moe, clarifying something he knew he did not need to.

"Thanks."

Jack had no desire to maintain such a conversation with a stranger. Without saying more, he sat in the driver seat and shut the door on Moe. Moe tapped his finger on the window, gently enough to be polite but firm enough to show assertiveness. Jack rolled it down, begrudgingly.

"We would like to talk to you. You guys can continue your business in Detroit but you're stepping on a lot of people's toes."

Jack was known for his short temper. He seemed to have

learned nothing from his erratic moments with Wilma. At work, one mistake that a worker would make on the line was followed by a verbal death sentence from Jack. It was this temper that caused Jack to make his next decision. He reached under the seat hastily and proceeded to exit the car, holding a 45 Automatic. He held the gun at his side and positioned his body right in front of Moe's. It was in that moment of anger and impulse when the light bulb went off in Jack's head. He remembered the man now.

"I remember you from the beauty shop. I'll tell you what. You see this 45. If you come around here again. I'm gonna blow your mother fucking head off."

Moe remained calm, cool, and collected. This obviously was not the first time he was threatened with a gun and he knew that Jack would never shoot someone in the parking lot in which he worked. He responded to this angst with a simple inquiry.

"Are you sure this is the answer you want to give the people I'm working with? They're not gonna like this."

Even though Jack was surprised that Moe's response did not seem to contain any fear or concern, Jack remained in what he felt like was control of the situation. He was the one with the weapon after all.

"You heard what I said," said Jack aggressively.

Jack got back into his car and drove off quickly, tires burning just as Moe lit a cigarette. It became a ritual for Moe. Although he did not project weakness, whenever anyone pulled a gun out on him, the best way for him to distress was to inhale tobacco and let the effects of nicotine take over his body. He looked forward to being the messenger of such controversial news, news that would result in dire consequences.

Later that day at Silverman's Cleaners, Wilma sat at the counter, daydreaming. Her mind drifted to when she was 18, and how the school bullies had put lemons in their mouths to try and sabotage her saxophone performance. She recalled that they were the first of many people in her life that would inflict wrongs upon her, simply because she was at the bottom of the social totem pole. She was a Negro woman. Once the term "Negro" came into her mind, she immediately thought of James Brown's song about having pride in being "black." She thought of how she needed to embrace that mentality and find the strength to no longer be a victim of her race. For a black woman, she had accomplished a lot after all.

Moe entered the cleaners, rapidly. He and Wilma made eye contact for a split second. Wilma always had trouble reading Moe. Ever since he delivered the towels from this very building to her shop on Linwood, Moe was always a mysterious fellow. He strolled passed the counter and went into Mr. Silverman's office. Seeing Moe reminded Wilma of her glory days at the shop.

It might be time to open a new salon, she thought.

Moe entered the office to see Mr. Silverman smoking a cigarette behind his desk. Mr. Hoffman stood in front of the desk and turned to face Moe. They were both anxiously waiting to hear about Moe's meeting with Jack.

"How's Jack doing?" asked Mr. Hoffman.

"He's fine but he pulled a 45 on me and said if I come around him again he's gonna blow my fucking head off."

The men's emotionless reactions were a testament to the

fact that such a threat was "just normal mob rhetoric." Moe lit a cigarette to calm himself down again. Mr. Silverman and Mr. Hoffman looked at each other, both contemplating their respective next comments and moves.

"Yeah, I had a feeling Jack was gonna be a problem," said Mr. Silverman almost disappointedly.

"Maybe it's time to send him a little message. I don't got time to waste on that nigger," said Mr. Hoffman assertively.

Mr. Silverman's comment was merely an opinionated observation whereas Mr. Hoffman's statement was far more inflammatory and decisive. Mr. Silverman had a feeling of where this conversation was going but he needed to be sure.

"What are we talking about, here?" asked Mr. Silverman.

Mr. Hoffman and Moe interpreted the question posed by Mr. Silverman as rhetorical, even though, Mr. Silverman desired a straight answer. He knew in his heart that what was coming was going to be tragic and what frustrated the man the most was that he had no control over the outcome.

I'm too old for this shit, he thought solemnly.

The Friday before Memorial Day was a day Wilma Bailey had off from work, which meant drinking began right as she woke up as opposed to after her long workday. She spent her morning playing her Billie Holiday record. When Ricky entered the living room, Wilma was singing along to "Summertime." Although her tipsiness disallowed her from nailing every note, Ricky still smiled for seeing his mother in good spirits. She had not reached that sad level of drunkenness yet. Ricky thought that calling off work to spend quality time with his mother would help curb her drinking but accumulating wealth for the next transition of his life was his main priority. He did however make sure she had enough food in her stomach to function for a days worth of alcohol intake.

"Want an omelet, Mama?" asked Ricky from the kitchen.

Wilma stopped singing to think about her response. The thought of Ricky's delicious breakfasts took over her mind.

"Who could say no to Ricky's famous omelets?"

Ricky stood over the stove and cooked the eggs. He sprinkled sharp cheddar cheese on top of the egg and sausage combination. Even with the window open, Ricky sweated profusely. Ricky ended up grabbing a Blatz Beer can from the fridge. He opened it, took a few sips, and put the can back in the fridge. Wilma watched Ricky's actions unfold from the living room couch.

"What the hell are you doing?" asked Wilma firmly.

"Making breakfast."

"If you're gonna open a beer, drink the whole can."

Even though Ricky was bulky, he knew drinking a whole beer before work would not be the best idea. Unlike his mother, he was a lightweight when it came to alcohol and got drunk very easily. The only reason Ricky opened that can was because he wanted something quick and cold to cool him off from the kitchen heat, but he would never tell his mother that.

"Okay, Mama."

Ricky grabbed the can out of the fridge as Wilma watched. He took a small sip and placed it on the counter and pretended to tend to the cooking of the eggs that were pretty much cooling down at that point. Once Wilma walked away and started singing again, Ricky dumped the rest of the beer down the sink.

One less thing for her to drink, thought Ricky.

Ricky served his "famous" omelet to his mother, which made her crack the biggest smile Ricky had seen in a long time. Wilma clearly enjoyed the food as she ate very quickly. Ricky decided then and there that he was going to cook for his mother more often. He loved making her happy.

A few hours after Ricky left for work, Wilma had finished her bottle of gin. She dazedly took the Billie Holiday record off and put on her favorite radio station, WJZZ before sprawling out on her bed and passing out.

At Clark Service Station, Ricky was very much awake as he pumped gasoline into a 1976 Cadillac Seville. Seeing cars like this humbled Ricky. He knew he would have to work hard and save money so he could one day have a ride as nice as this. Ricky made eye contact with the driver as he pumped gas. The face was very familiar and it took Ricky a minute before realizing it was Shirley's husband, Jerry. Jerry did not recognize nor bother to acknowledge Ricky. Ricky wasn't feeling particularly enthused to force small talk with a man he barely knew. He kept to himself as he did his job.

Wilma's alcoholism had indeed alienated herself from her family but it was her relative's constant admiration of the fallen John L., which rubbed Wilma the wrong way. It had been ten years since John L.'s scam and Wilma had kept it from her family. It was an embarrassing occurrence and she feared how her 79-year-old father Harry would react if he found out his favorite nephew had used and abused his daughter. The shock might be too much for his heart to handle.

The same sentiment was felt for Bobby Hunt, whose treatment of Wilma, was betrayal in the purest form. Then again, it was harder to hate Bobby Hunt on the same level of John L. because Wilma had witnessed firsthand how drugs morphed people into unfamiliar monsters. Because of Wilma's dichotomy with her family, she did not keep in touch with them too often. Bunny, Claireece, and Harry decided to spend the patriotic holiday weekend to pay their respects to their favorite veteran. At

Elmwood Cemetery, Bunny led the way as Claireece gripped the handles of Harry's wheelchair. Harry held a folded American flag tightly in his arms as his wife pushed him. They moseyed along the paved path until Bunny finally spotted the gravestone they were searching for. Claireece suggested for the spryer Bunny to forcefully push Harry's wheelchair across the coarse grass. This was a minuscule test of strength considering the training she went through for the Navy. Claireece grabbed the flag from Harry and placed it in front of a grave that read: "Here Lies: John Lovington Miller 1925-1966: An American Soldier of the Korean War."

John L.'s body had never been found since his disappearance in 1966. It was not until a couple years ago when the Miller/Bailey family decided to accept the fact that John L. was gone and to honor his memory by giving him a gravestone. Although the family was not as aware of John L.'s shadiness like Wilma, they knew that the "gangster lifestyle" he had made for himself did not yield itself to be a safe existence. Harry was the most stubborn one to believe in the man that served his country and not the Gorilla Pimp Detroit had turned him into. The three family members stood silent before walking away, somberly.

The family could only begin to understand the meaning of somber at that point. Wilma's somber mood led her to knock back an entire bottle of Seagram's before sunset. Her drunken stupor did not allow her to hear the knock on her front door that Friday evening. Instead she was sprawled out on her bed, passed out. Without the knocker saying a word, the front door opened quietly and slowly. Like most homeowners of the time, locking the door was not customary. The mysterious intruder entered the home. He definitely was not an expected guest.

He skulked around the kitchen, looking for something specific. Wearing black leather gloves, the man reached for the stove and firmly grasped Wilma's cast iron skillet. It was the same iron cast skillet that Ricky had cooked pineapple upside down cake, macaroni and cheese, and cornbread since the 60s. Holding the skillet to his side, the figure slowly walked into the living room and soaked up Wilma's apartment. The messiness bothered him but he enjoyed the faint music he heard emanating from the nearby radio. He decided to turn the knob to increase the decibel level of the music. "I Loves You, Porgy" by Nina Simone was now quite audible.

In that moment on the other side of town, Mr. Silverman was having a barbecue at his Sherwood Forest Mansion. Friends, businessmen, and family all came together to get a taste of Silverman's grilled steaks. Mr. Hoffman resented Mr. Silverman for not attending the Union Dinner that night, but Mr. Silverman chose to enjoy himself. His enjoyment was dampened, however, by not seeing a certain guest at the barbecue. The absentee guest had become a staple in Mr. Silverman's life. As he grilled, he started daydreaming about the past. He looked out on his large backyard at the sea of people socializing and just waited for that guest to come strolling in, the sun bouncing off of the blonde streak in her hair. Even though Mr. Silverman invited Wilma, he knew in his heart that she was not coming.

"Max..." said Mrs. Silverman.

Mr. Silverman snapped out of his daze and made eye contact with his wife.

"What?" he asked as he wiped sweat from his forehead.

"You're burning the steaks..."

At Cobo Hall, there was a Union dinner of three hundred members all seated at their respective round tables. When Mr. Hoffman commanded the stage, applause erupted loudly. Some of the members in that room knew the kind of man Mr. Hoffman was but most of them only saw him as a virtuous and competent leader. There would only be whispers of his involvement with organized crime. These whispers would die as they left the mouths of the members. For they knew, even if he was an integral part of the mob, he still was their President and strived to make their lives easier. Mr. Hoffman's opening remarks echoed the tone of one Alabama Governor many years before.

"Solidarity today, solidarity tomorrow, solidarity forever!"

Right as Mr. Hoffman's words hit a fever pitch, Wilma's intruder repeatedly hit Wilma in the head with the cast iron skillet. Blood and brain matter splattered all over the bed in which she lay and stained the violet walls of her home. The bloody skillet was then dropped by the bed, next to her frequently used vinyl styling bag that was underneath. The perpetrator turned the melancholy music of Nina Simone back down and left the apartment.

Later that night, Jerry went to pick up Shirley to go Baker's Jazz Club. After a long week on the street, they were both excited to have a night out to enjoy themselves and relax. That journey was unfortunately cut short. On the corner of Woodward and Seven Mile, Jerry was pulled over by a police car, strategically hidden behind some bushes. Jerry's initial instinct was to speed away, but Shirley begged for him to pull the car to the side of the road. They were only going five over after all. A white officer approached the drivers side of the vehicle while a black cop walked toward Shirley's side. Once the officers arrived at the car, Jerry rolled down the window and Shirley followed suit.

"Is there a problem, officer?" asked Jerry calmly.

"In a hurry? You were driving pretty fast," the white cop said.

"I was always told I have a lead foot," Jerry joked.

The officer was not amused and made eye contact with a silent Shirley and then the black cop through the open window. The black cop surveyed the back seat and gazed upon a small plastic bag, partially covered by the upholstery. Before even acknowledging his partner, the black officer made his own command.

"I'm gonna have to ask both of you to step out of the vehicle please."

The white officer was skeptical but followed his partner's lead. Jerry and Shirley nervously complied. They exited the vehicle slowly. In that moment, the black officer handcuffed Shirley and started dragging her to the police car.

"No! No! Let go of me!" shrieked Shirley.

Jerry began to jolt to the other side of the vehicle to rescue his wife, but the white officer slammed Jerry up against the car and handcuffed him as well. They both were thrown in the back of the police car and neither of their rights were read. The officers opened the doors to the back seat of the Seville and discovered a small package of heroin neatly covered by tightly folded paper. The white officer pocketed the heroin.

At Clark Service Station, the owner of the establishment, Mr. Rice, exited the store with Ricky following behind. Mr. Rice was a short black man with a bushy mustache. He compensated for his height with his deep voice. The reason the men left the shop was because a police car pulled into the lot and parked. It appeared that answers were needed instead of gasoline. The question was how much more flammable one was compared to the other. Wilma's old admirer, Lester came out of the passenger seat, wearing a beige suit as opposed to a regular police uniform. His partner, Patrick Flanagan, was dressed similarly, but waited in the car.

"Who is the owner here?" asked Lester.

"I'm the owner," responded Mr. Rice.

"And you're Ricky?" Lester asked as he made eye contact with his old flame's son.

"Yeah."

Ricky did not feel the need to remind the man that they knew each other from past occurrences and neither did Lester, especially now.

"I'm Detective Lester Cunningham. I work for the Detroit Police Department. I'm gonna need to ask you some questions but for the record, can you state your full name for me."

Lester got straight to business. He placed his pen up to his notepad and waited for Ricky's response. Ricky hesitantly answered, unsure of what this was all about.

"Frederick Norment."

"You have a middle name, Frederick?"

"Charles."

"Frederick Charles Norment?" Lester asked, for clarification.

"Yes."

"I'm gonna ask you to sit in the car with Detective Flanagan so I can ask your boss a few questions."

Ricky was taken aback by this comment. He knew they could not arrest him for anything, but he had never been in the back of a cop car before. The thought made him uncomfortable, but he knew compliance would only get the answers he was looking for, more quickly.

"Okay," replied Ricky.

Lester opened the rear door on the passenger side and Ricky got in.

"What's this about?" asked Mr. Rice.

"Mr. Rice, have you worked with Ricky all day today?"

"Yes. He's been here all day."

"Did he go home for lunch?"

"No we had sandwiches here, actually."

If there was one thing Lester needed right now it was certainty.

"Are you sure?" Lester asked firmly.

"Yes, I'm sure," said Mr. Rice confidently.

"Can you walk over to the car with me, please?" asked Lester.

Mr. Rice nodded and Lester led them back to the police car. Lester opened the back door so now Ricky could be part of the conversation again. A conversation he would never forget. Lester had debated during the entire car ride how he was going to break the news to Ricky. Instead of splitting the content up like he planned to, what had spewed out his mouth was all of the information at once. It was not the most cohesive delivery, but all that mattered was that Ricky received the news he needed to hear.

"Ricky, I have some bad news for you. I'm from homicide and around 5 o'clock today your mother was murdered. She was beaten to death with a blunt object."

"Oh my God," blurted out Mr. Rice.

Ricky stared blankly into the rear view mirror of the police car. In the mirror he saw a homeless man on the corner begging for money. Ricky had noticed him a few times before on his way to work and would sometimes give him some change. Ricky secretly hoped the money he gave the man would go to bettering his life, but in that moment, Ricky witnessed the man take a swig from a flask he kept in his raggedy coat. This man was not the only alcoholic he had enabled. This initially made Ricky feel guilty until he processed that this was a murder, not because she drank too much. His guilt turned to anger at whoever could do such an atrocious act. His anger subsided when he remembered his mother's pain. He recalled many of the terrible things she went through in order to give himself and Ronnie a good life. He internalized this emotional journey flawlessly.

"Are you okay?" asked Patrick.

"I'm all right," said Ricky calmly.

"Ricky, take all the time you need. Come back when you're ready. Your job will be here for you," said Mr. Rice.

Ricky nodded slowly, clearly in his own head. Lester shook Mr. Rice's hand.

"Thank you for your help," said Lester.

Mr. Rice nodded and walked back into the store. The car left the station with Ricky still inside. He did not even process that the car was moving.

"Did you want to go back to the house and pick up some things?" asked Lester.

Ricky's hands trembled before he answered. Although his Varsity Jacket was the most important item in the house, he had no desire to go in there or even touch anything that was in there.

"No," Ricky said quietly.

"Guess who got the lead on this case?" asked Patrick.

"Who?" inquired Lester.

"Greene."

"Are you serious?" asked Lester incredulously.

"Yeah. He just came off suspension."

"Wow. Sounds like bullshit to me."

Although Ricky's thoughts were louder than the words of those men, he did piece together that whoever was handling this case did not seem like a good choice.

Why was he suspended? Who killed my mother? thought Ricky.

Chapter 25: Summer 1976

The Green Leaf Restaurant was relatively empty with only a few tables filled. Old ceiling fans rotated slowly to keep the patrons only moderately cool from the scorching June heat. Waiters and waitresses moved in the background, delivering meals to their respective tables. Mr. Silverman and Moe sat across from each other at a table in the corner. Mr. Silverman loosened his tie out of discomfort from the heat. He then proceeded to unwrap the napkin from his utensils to wipe the sweat from his brow. Moe, on the other hand, sat comfortably and still as he studied the menu intently. Mr. Silverman stared at Moe until Moe raised his head after feeling the fire in the old man's eyes.

"How the fuck are you gonna pull the trigger on Wilma and not tell me?" asked Mr. Silverman disdainfully.

Moe's brief moment of eye contact ended after processing the inquiry. His vision returned to the menu but his words conveyed were far less appetizing.

"Hoffman's orders. Not mine."

"It was unnecessary and reckless," said Mr. Silverman with conviction.

Now Moe interpreted the conversation to be more important than his lunch selection.

"Unnecessary? Are you fucking kidding me? The fucker almost killed me in the parking lot," retorted Moe sternly yet quietly.

"That was Jack. Wilma didn't deserve this."

For the first time, Mr. Silverman revealed his sympathy to his cohort. It was sympathy for a woman he grew to respect and admire. It was just tragic that such sympathy could not prevent what had happened.

"If word got out that we were soft on Progressive 11, all the fuckers wouldn't take us seriously."

Moe's explanation would never be enough of a justification to murder a defenseless woman. Wilma went through hell and back for her children only to be taken out because of an organization she unknowingly sacrificed her life for. Mr. Silverman had no intention of letting Moe off easy and interjected.

"Well..."

Moe wasn't going to let Mr. Silverman off easy either.

"Look Max, you got a problem take it up with Hoffman."

Mr. Silverman chuckled to himself. It seemed that laughter was the only way to cope with the grave truth. It was an undeniable fact that Hoffman ran Detroit. Mr. Silverman knew that any objection to his motives would cause him to end up just like Wilma: bankrupt and dead.

"What'll it be, gentlemen?" asked the newly arrived waitress.

Mr. Silverman could not help but smirk at how she referred himself and Moe. Such a common and colloquial term was used so frequently but at times did not apply. Mr. Silverman did not consider Moe a "gentle" man by any means. In the end, neither was he.

"Burger and fries for me," blurted out Moe.

Moe handed the waitress the menu with a decisive gesture. She instinctively grabbed it and turned her body to Mr.

Silverman.

"And for you?"

Mr. Silverman did not glance once at the menu that laid in front of him. He made eye contact with the waitress and turned his sights to Moe. While glaring at Moe, he responded to the waitress.

"Nothing. I just lost my appetite."

Mr. Silverman stood up and walked out of the restaurant. He needed to grieve his friend's death in his own way.

There was no place more beautiful than Belle Isle at sunset, especially during the summer. The way the dimming sun reflected off of the Detroit River, coupled with the silence of nature made it the ideal choice for Jack to meet his Progressive 11 business partner. It was the prefect place to get away and think. That's what Jack had done for the past three hours as he sat in his Impala and waited for his friend near the bank of the river. A 1975 Ford LTD pulled up next to Jack's car. Benny exited his vehicle and walked up to Jack's passenger door. Benny opened the door and sat down in the passenger seat.

"I like the view, but why are we meeting here?"

Jack had a million thoughts racing through his head. He had remained pensive and calm by himself for the past few hours but once Benny entered his car, he could only think of one phrase that summed up everything concisely.

"It's over."

This response was to the point but not enough to satisfy Benny's curiosity.

"Why? What are you talking about?" asked Benny.

"Wilma's death wasn't random. It was a message to us."

Benny had heard about Wilma's untimely death. He initially assumed her alcoholism finally got the best of her, but once he was told she was murdered, it did cause him to wonder who would do such a heinous act. Benny would have never thought to connect the killing to his business with Jack. Sure, they were not the most likeable group in Detroit, but to murder someone over it was a big pill to swallow. Benny felt the need to try and convince Jack otherwise.

"But Jack..."

Jack refused to cater to Benny's naivety, not tonight. He cut him off quickly and smoothly.

"Make sure everyone gets this," interrupted Jack.

Jack pulled out a large stack of envelopes from his jacket.

"These are their initial investments with interest," said Jack flatly.

Jack handed Benny the envelopes. As Benny grabbed them hesitantly, Jack put his hands on top of Benny's, firmly. He looked him in eye and Benny could tell Jack was scared. He could see the fear seeping out of his eyes. Benny had never seen Jack like this before.

"I don't want anyone else to get hurt," said Jack sincerely.

Benny reassessed the possibility of Wilma's murder relating to Progressive 11 and how much the company had stepped on mob toes. He figured that an argument with Jack would be futile and had to accept in his heart that their organization would no longer be active. Although Wilma was Jack's ex-wife, he knew Jack well enough to know that Wilma was the love of his life. Jack had just realized it too late. Benny's thoughts of Wilma shifted to concern about Jack's next step.

"When are you coming back to the plant?"

"I gotta help Ricky and Ronnie bury their mom. I'll be back next week."

"Progressive 11. It could have been really big."

Jack knew Benny's comment was a veiled attempt to make Jack feel guilty for disbanding the organization. Benny was right about the potential that Progressive 11 had, but the sarcastic tone in which he said it, was not appreciated. Jack chose to call attention to the wealth Benny had already accumulated.

"Benny, you ain't hurtin' for nothing."

Benny made good money and so did Jack. Benny felt the need to include Jack in that commentary.

"I guess we did all right," said Benny.

Benny waited for Jack to have a change of heart and reconsider the longevity of Progressive 11. Jack's heart would never be the same. As much as he was in the long haul with Edna, Wilma would always be considered "the one that got away." Much like Wilma's had been years prior, Jack's entrepreneurial spirit had been crushed. This painful thought prompted Jack to end the interaction with his old friend, who would keep asking questions, or say some things that would only add fuel to the already scorching wildfire burning inside of him.

"Okay, Benny. I gotta go. I'll talk to you later."

Jack's comment was preceded by Jack motioning his head toward the passenger door. This was the signal to "get out."

"I think I'm gonna wait in my car for a few more minutes. It's peaceful out here," said Benny.

Benny's eyes peered through Jack's dirty windshield and out to the pinkish and orange sky, which was the most beautiful sight he had seen in awhile, this excluded his wife of course. Just as Benny exited the car, Jack turned his engine and sped off of the grass and onto the road leading him back inland. All he could think about was how envious of Benny he was with regards to calling Belle Isle "peaceful." As much as Jack wanted to find peace that night, he had to come to terms with the terrible truth that he would never be at peace knowing that his business may have factored into Wilma's death.

Judge Hamilton, an older white man with short graying black hair, entered the stuffy courtroom. He walked passed an obese Bailiff who stood straight and had an expression that conveyed that he took his job too seriously.

"All rise for the honorable Judge C. Hamilton. Court is now in session," declared the Bailiff.

Everyone in the courtroom stood up as Judge Hamilton took the bench. Ricky and Ronnie were among the patrons and they stared menacingly at the defendant, Jerry. Jerry made eye contact with the boys only for a brief moment, but it was long enough to absorb their disdain. Jerry's white lawyer, Mr. Richardson, put his hand on Jerry's shoulder, attempting to loosen him up. Next to Ricky and Ronnie, stood the Assistant D.A.; Mr. Beamon. He was a tall white man who wore dark rimmed glasses that complemented his big brown eyes quite well. His suit was a little too tight for him, which made sense for a man constantly referred to as; "uptight." Mr. Beamon leaned in closer to the boys.

"We did everything we could," he said softly.

From his outside observations and his own personal experiences, Ronnie tended to be cynical of the law and its enforcers. Mr. Beamon's comment did not surprise Ronnie as much as it did Ricky. Ricky remained hopeful that the murderer of her mother would receive justice, but Mr. Beamon's tone said otherwise.

"Everyone can be seated," said the Bailiff.

Jack entered the courtroom slowly, to avoid his son seeing him. He took a seat in the back seating area. He noticed Ricky from afar. It made him happy to see his son whom he had not seen in months, but he feared Ricky would resent him for his mother's death. Jack contemplated if Ricky understood the complexity of the case and knew that Jerry was just a patsy. Jack could only hope that the court understood that as well.

"Counsel, can you please approach the bench," said Judge Hamilton in a deep and booming voice.

Mr. Beamon and Mr. Richardson advanced to the bench quickly. It was if they partook in a subtle competition in those few seconds as to who would approach the bench first. But the real game was this case, a case that, according to Judge Hamilton, should have never played out this way.

"I'm upset that you're wasting my time and the people's money. Beamon, you should have known this," Judge Hamilton said sternly.

Mr. Beamon had an idea of what the judge was talking about, but like any lawyer, he craved specificity.

"What's going on?"

"If you would have interviewed Detective Greene more carefully, this wouldn't have to happen. Richardson, I'm going to grant your motion. Now get out of my face so I can finish this."

Mr. Beamon and Mr. Richardson returned to their seats. Mr. Richardson beat Mr. Beamon there. As the men sat, Judge Hamilton's loud and baritone voice projected into the courtroom.

"Considering that there is not sufficient evidence against the defendant, and that he was questioned at the police station multiple times without being arrested nor mirandized, this is in direct violation of his Civil Rights. I cannot take this to trial. Case dismissed."

Judge Hamilton banged the gavel slicing through the silence of the courtroom. Amazement and befuddlement were the common reactions from the patrons. Judge Hamilton exited the side door just as Mr. Richardson rushed Jerry out of the courtroom for fear of Wilma's confidants causing him harm. Everyone else got up to leave. Janette, Kathy, Anita, and Doris sat in the same row and solemnly migrated together. Each woman was close to Wilma, but Kathy had always considered Wilma to be a maternal figure in her life. Tears streamed down her face after the gavel had banged down on the metaphorical nail in the coffin. It was that jarring noise that really made Kathy realize that her role model was gone.

Ricky sat there and reflected on the type of person his mother was. She was someone who was loved by many. He looked around and saw many people holding back tears in their eyes, mourning not only for Wilma, but also for the blatant lack of justice that had just been displayed. Ricky could not believe the verdict. Legislation that had been fought so long and tirelessly by the African American community was actually used against his family because the accused was black. Mr. Beamon turned to a motionless Ricky.

"Ricky, we just need to do some follow-up questions in the back."

Ricky nodded slowly as he processed the information coming out of Mr. Beamon's mouth. He nodded to Ronnie to convey that he was okay and followed Mr. Beamon to the back of the courtroom, walking like a zombie.

Mr. Beamon and Ricky entered the Judge's Chamber, but instead of seeing Old Man Hamilton, Ricky gazed upon a beautiful middle-aged blonde woman in a navy blue suit. Dr. Dodds sat at a table with her hands crossed and had a cheerful disposition. Her demeanor contrasted Ricky's current mood starkly.

"Ricky, this is Dr. Dodds. She's a counselor who has a few questions for you before you leave," said Mr. Beamon.

Ricky and Dr. Dodds made eye contact and then Ricky nodded to Mr. Beamon to express his understanding. Mr. Beamon pulled out a chair for Ricky. Ricky sat down and faced

Dr. Dodds. Ricky hoped the exchange would be quick for he thought "shrinks" were for crazy people.

"I'll be right outside if you need anything," said Mr. Beamon.

In Ricky's head he wanted to say that he would never need anything from him ever again, but the polite response was uttered instead.

"Thanks."

Mr. Beamon exited the room, giving a subtle head nod to Dr. Dodds, which translated to: "he's all yours." Dr. Dodds studied Ricky for a few seconds before commenting on the case.

"That verdict must be hard for you to accept."

Ricky never enjoyed people telling him how he should feel. That's all growing up was. Ricky wanted to get straight to the point.

"What do you want to talk to me about?"

"First off, how are you feeling?" asked Dr. Dodds.

What a loaded question, he thought.

His mother was dead and her perpetrator was not given

the justice he deserved, whether it was Jerry or not. He wanted someone to pay the price but it looked like no one was going to. Wilma Bailey would just be another dead black person no one cared about.

How could some rich white woman fathom this pain, he thought.

"Fine," said Ricky curtly.

"Ricky, this is a lot to take in at once. You can talk to me about it."

Dr. Dodds's response seemed robotic and disingenuous. It was the kind of response that was probably drilled into her head in college in order to make a patient feel more comfortable. Ricky did not trust the strange woman and had no intention of unleashing his inner demons upon her. She probably could not handle it.

"I have nothing to say," said Ricky.

"I want to make sure you don't let this build up. I don't want you to hurt yourself...or hurt anybody else..."

Ricky then put the pieces together. This meeting was less

about his mental state and more about addressing the fear of what a young angry black man was going to do now that his poor old mother was dead. Ricky was offended at the assumption that he would hurt people but he figured it was not worth bringing up. He and this "counselor" were clearly on two different wavelengths. He decided to be cordial just in case she was actually concerned about his well-being.

"I won't."

Dr. Dodds looked over her notes almost as a filler to pass time and make the situation a little less awkward. She did however come across a tidbit of information that she hoped would keep the current "one-sided" conversation going.

"You not showing any emotion troubles me. And it says in the police report that you didn't show any emotion when they informed you of your mother's death. Why is that?"

Ricky sat there silent for a good 30 seconds before answering.

"I can't cry no more. I've been crying all my life for my Mom. She's in a better place now. She can finally get some rest."

Epilogue

Since the Civil Rights Movement, entrepreneurship in Detroit plummeted. Out of all of the neighborhood businesses, Davis Brothers Gas Station is the only one that is black owned. Much like Wilma Bailey, Detroit became bankrupt and dead.

For the cosmetology market in Detroit, an epicenter as popular as Bailey's Salon would never exist again. Kim went on to be apart of a 3 billion dollar a year industry, in which, the synthetic wig and weave market became dominated by Korean Americans. This was another industry that slipped through the fingers of the African American entrepreneurs.

Jack married Edna but never had more children. He retired from General Motors and made amends with his only son, Ricky, a year after Wilma's death. Wilma Bailey was buried on June 6, 1976. To this day, her killer has not been exposed nor put to justice. Ricky thinks about his mother every day and because of her guidance, he became a Professional Chef. He married in 1989 and has a 23-year-old daughter. He lives with his wife in Ann Arbor, Michigan.